Crafting with
Vellum & Parchment
New & Exciting Paper Projects

Crafting with
Vellum & Parchment

New & Exciting Paper Projects

Marie Browning

Sterling Publishing Co., Inc.
New York

Prolific Impressions Production Staff:

Editor: Mickey Baskett
Copy: Phyllis Mueller
Graphics: Dianne Miller, Karen Turpin
Styling: Lenos Key
Photography: Pat Molnar
Administration: Jim Baskett

Library of Congress Cataloging-in-Publication Data Available

Published by Sterling Publishing Company, Inc.
387 Park Avenue South, New York, N.Y. 10016
Produced by Prolific Impressions, Inc.
160 South Candler St., Decatur, GA 30030
©2001 Prolific Impressions, Inc.
Distributed in Canada by Sterling Publishing
c/o Canadian Manda Group, One Atlantic Avenue, Suite 105
Toronto, Ontario, Canada M6K 3E7
Distributed in Great Britain and Europe by Cassell PLC
Wellington House, 125 Strand, London WC2R 0BB, England
Distributed in Australia by Capricorn Link (Australia) Pty. Ltd.
P.O. Box 6651, Baulkham Hills, Business Centre, NSW 2153 Australia

Printed in China
All rights reserved
Sterling ISBN #0-8069-2971-5

ACKNOWLEDGMENTS

Marie Browning thanks the following manufactures for their generous contributions of materials used in this book:

Clearsnap, Inc.
http://www.clearsnap.com
Waterproof dye inkpads, roller stamps, rubber stamps

CTI Paper USA, Inc.
Sun Prairie, Wisconsin, USA
Large selection of high quality European parchments, vellums, envelopes

Eagle OPG Inc.
http://www.holdthatthought.com
Decorative poly (vellum-like) gift bags, boxes, gift packages

Ecstasy Crafts
http://www.ecstasycraft.com
Books, patterns, quality parchment papers, rainbow parchments, embossing and piercing tools, coloring systems for parchment, window cards

Fiskars
http://www.fiskars.com
Decorative scissors, slide trimmer, art knives, cutting mats

Grafix
http://www.grafixarts.com
Double-sided adhesive mounting film, laminate film, large selection of specialty papers

Loose Ends
http://www.looseends.com
Wide selection of decorative papers, skeleton leaves, decorative accessories

Nature's Pressed
http://www.naturespressed.com
Professionally pressed flowers, leaves, greenery

The Paper Company
http://www.thepaperco.com
Colored and printed vellums and vellum envelopes

Papers By Catherine
Houston, Texas, USA
Handmade and decorative papers including embossed vellum panels, printed and colored vellums

Personal Stamp Exchange
http://www.psxstamps.com
Rubber stamps and stamping accessories including box templates, thermal embossing powders, ink pads, window cards, vellum, parchment papers

Therm O Web
http://www.thermoweb.com
Mounting adhesive, double-sided tapes, laminating sheets

Toybox Rubber Stamps
Healdsburg, California, USA
Beautiful rubber stamps

Yasutomo Gel Xtreme Pens
San Francisco, California, USA
Gel metallic, white, and colored pens that work on parchment and vellum papers

About the Author
MARIE BROWNING

Marie Browning is a consummate craft designer, making a career of designing products, writing books and articles, plus teaching and demonstrating. You may have already been charmed by her creative designs and not even been aware; as she has designed stencils, stamps, transfers, and a variety of other products for national art & craft supply companies.

You may also have enjoyed Marie's popular book entitled, *Beautiful Handmade Natural Soaps* published by Sterling Publishing in 1998. In addition to soapmaking, Marie has authored several other books published by Sterling, *Handcrafted Journals, Albums, Scrapbooks, & More* (1999), *Gifts From Your Garden* (1999), and *Memory Gifts* (2000). Her articles and designs have appeared in *Handcraft Illustrated*, *Better Homes & Gardens*, *Canadian Stamper*, *Great American Crafts*, *All American Crafts*, and in numerous project books published by Plaid Enterprises, Inc.

Browning earned a Fine Arts Diploma from Camosun College and attended the University of Victoria. She is a Certified Professional Demonstrator, a professional affiliate of the Canadian Craft and Hobby Association, and a member of the Stencil Artisan's League and the Society of Craft Designers.

Marie Browning lives, gardens, and crafts on Vancouver Island in Canada. She and her husband Scott have three children: Katelyn, Lena, and Jonathan. Marie can be contacted at: www.mariebrowning.com.

Paper crafts are seeing a renewed popularity. Working with parchment and vellum are a large part of this popular paper crafting trend. This book presents techniques and projects that showcase the exquisite qualities of parchment and vellum papers. You're probably familiar with parchment and vellum because they have long been used for wedding invitations and flyleaves in books, but you may not be aware of how wonderful they are as crafting papers.

Parchment and vellum were originally created with animal hides, but today a wide variety of "vegetarian" parchment and vellum papers – made with plant fibers – are available. Paper pulp parchments and vellums have the fine qualities of real parchments, whether they have a soft mottled pattern, a translucent quality, or a smooth, fine surface. Parchment and vellum have the strength to hold up to intricate piercing and cutting and the hardness to hold clean, crisp folds. The beauty of the smooth, translucent surface glows under light when used for lampshade and luminary construction.

Techniques in this book include the beautiful art of paper filigree lace craft, with roots reaching back to nuns in convents at the time of Christopher Columbus, the Victorian art of paper pricking, vellum weaving, paper folding, and crafting with natural materials. Many techniques require only paper, simple tools and a clean, brightly lit work space. Much of my inspiration for the parchment lace crafting patterns in this book were inspired from actual pieces of antique lace as shown in the photo on this page.

Projects that can be created with parchment and vellum are practically unlimited. I have included examples of cards, lanterns, luminaries, candle shades, packaging, ornaments, and tabletop and wall decorations.

Contents

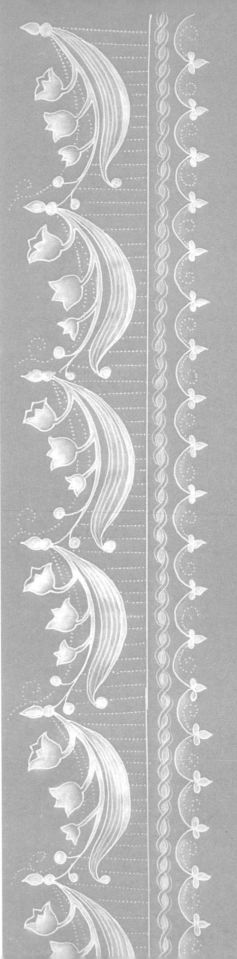

Historically,
parchment has been used for calligraphy, bookbinding, important documents, and fine art. Art and documents created on parchment convey importance, quality, and excellence. Although there are hundreds of types of paper available today, parchment remains the best choice for beauty, performance, and longevity.

True parchment is derived from goat and sheep hides; finer vellum is made from calfskin. Real parchment and vellum are still made today according to medieval recipes and are used for fine bookbinding, important documents and manuscripts, restoring ancient works, and fine art calligraphy and illuminated works. Real parchment costs $9 to $65 a square foot. Today's "vegetarian" or "imitation" parchment and vellum papers are produced on machines with plant fibers and come in a great abundance of weights, colors, transparencies, and designs and cost considerably less.

The name "parchment" is derived from *Pergamum,* the Latin name for the town of Bergama in western Turkey where parchment was developed to replace papyrus in the second century B.C. King Eumenes II wanted to create a library as complete as the library at Alexandria but could not acquire the papyrus needed to produce manuscripts. He substituted parchment, and soon parchment replaced papyrus as the chief writing material. A few parchment manuscripts, including the Dead Sea scrolls, survive from this early period.

In 105 A.D. in the Chinese emperor's court an imperial guard, Ts'ai Lun, made the first paper of plant fibers. Paper made from plants was soon to replace papyrus, silk, parchment, and vellum as a less costly and more accessible source of writing material in the East. Parchment was the preferred material for illuminated manuscripts, some of the finest pieces of art to come out of the Middle Ages. These manuscripts were hand lettered, tinted with rich colors, and highlighted with gold and silver leaf. Paper replaced parchment in the West with the advent of printing, when Johannes Gutenberg invented movable type in 1438.

In Spain, the Moorish conquerors brought parchment crafting during their occupation. Beautiful, prized bobbin lace, handmade by nuns in convents before the advent of machine-made lace, was produced on a pillow using a pricked-out parchment pattern.

When missionaries accompanied the Spanish conquistadors, the craft was brought to South America and gradually spread throughout the new world. Colombian, Peruvian, Argentine, and Brazilian artists developed unique styles.

The tremendous popularity of parchment craft today is due largely to the efforts of one woman, Martha Ospina, who brought the craft to The Netherlands when she moved there from her native Columbia in 1987. She taught parchment crafting there to increase her social circle and learn the Dutch language. "Pergamano," the trade name of the Colombian method that Ospina helped develop, is used as a general term for parchment lace crafting today. In Puerto Rico, parchment crafting is known as *tarjeteria pergaminada,* which means "the art of making greeting cards using parchment paper." The tarjeteria style, which generally does not include intricate cutting techniques, is also well known.

Embossed and pierced parchment designs, which I refer to as "Parchment Lace"

Antique greeting cards that use parchment.

in this book, look very detailed, but the basic processes are quite simple. The techniques traditionally used in parchment lace crafting of the "Pergamano®" method include tracing the design, pressure embossing, coloring, piercing, perforating, and cutting. Modern additions include coloring techniques with ink, paint, and oil crayons, dorsing (coloring from the back) and 3-D effects.

Parchment or Vellum?

Real parchment and vellum are paper-like materials prepared from raw, untreated animal skins that have been de-haired and dried under tension. Almost any animal skin can be used to create parchment, but sheep, goat, and calf hides are most commonly used. The term "vellum" is reserved for parchment made from calfskin. The word vellum (and the French *velin*) are derived from *vitellus*, the Latin word for calf. Parchment was named for the city of Pergamum, where it was invented, and the Latin *Pathica pellis*, meaning "Parthian skin."

More accurate terms for the papers we see today might be "imitation vellum" or "imitation parchment." Modern imitation vellum and parchment papers are manufactured from wood pulp on machines.

Vellum-like papers can be made two ways. Good quality European imitation parchment and vellum are made by beating the fibers for a very long time, until they are transparent – hence the name for the process, transparentization. No chemical sizing is added, and the resulting paper is pH balanced and safe for crafting. In the second method, chemical transparentization, wood pulp is beaten and petroleum-based resins are added. The resins act like

grease on the paper and make it translucent. (This also explains its strong solvent-like scent.)

Modern parchment and vellum papers differ in texture, opacity, and weight. Manufacturers use a variety of terms and definitions, and there is much confusion about these terms. Nowadays, it seems that any mottled, smooth, finely textured, or slightly translucent paper is called parchment or vellum. In this book, I use the term "parchment" generically to describe mottled, opaque, and translucent heavier papers and use the term "vellum" to describe finer, lighter weight translucent papers.

Parchment lace crafting (such as "Pergamano®") uses a heavyweight parchment-like paper that is manufactured in Europe without strong chemicals. The proper weight is 140/150g, and it must be strong enough to take the pressure embossing without cracking. The paper simulates all the qualities of a real animal skin parchment, which turns a satiny white when pressure embossed and can hold up to fine perforating and lace-like cutting treatments.

The imitation vellum papers available to crafters are much too lightweight for embossing or perforating, but they are wonderful for backing parchment craft work or creating overlays for cards. ❏

𝒫apers

There are a wide variety of parchment and vellum papers available today because of the popularity of paper crafting. Following are some types that you will find available in art, craft, print and stationery stops.

Opaque Parchment Papers

A variety of mottled, opaque papers are generally used for printing and photocopying. They range in weight from a lighter 20 lb. bond for general printing use and 40 to 60 lb. heavier card weight for covers. They come in a variety of light colors, from creams and tans to greens and blues and are available in letter and legal size pages and 22" x 30" sheets. When you ask at an art or craft supply store or print shop for parchment paper, this is generally what you will be shown.

Translucent Parchment Papers

Translucent papers have the same mottled appearance but are translucent. They come in a variety of weights, from 20 lb. to 60 lb., in a selection of whites, creams, rainbow, and marbled hues. They make beautiful luminaries and lampshades. Parchment lace craft parchments are available in a variety of suitable weights, sizes, and colors. You also can find pre-printed parchment strips (generally butterflies and flowers) designed for three-dimensional designs.

Vellum Papers

There is a wide selection of vellum papers. They are generally very light in weight and translucent. They can be used for soft, muted effects on a memory page, as a surface for a rubber stamped card, for making folded ornaments, or for constructing a translucent lampshade.

Pre-embossed vellum panels, vellums embedded with metallic sprinkles, and vellums with a subtle line pattern formed when the paper was made on a screen (called a "laid" finish) are available.

Colored vellums capture all the hues of the rainbow, plus black and metallics.

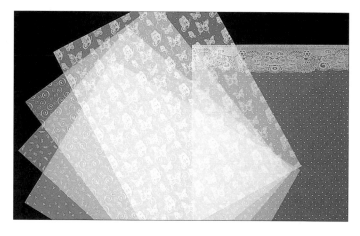

Printed Vellum

A wide variety of printed vellums are available. Designs printed with white ink on the translucent vellum imitate the soft, muted effects of embossing and are best shown with a colored sheet in behind them. Vellums printed with colored inks can be subtle or bold, elegant or whimsical.

Plain and colored vellums also can be purchased with gold embossed designs. The effect can be achieved with rubber stamps and thermal embossing with much more work and time.

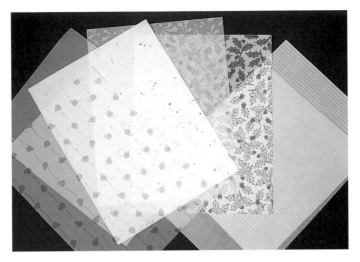

Vellum Envelopes

Vellum envelopes are beautiful companions to handcrafted vellum cards and elegant parchment invitations. They also are wonderful for creating books with translucent pages or elegant scented sachets for a lady's lingerie drawer.

Storing Paper

Paper must be kept clean and crisp. Store your paper flat and neatly to prevent wrinkling and folding. Folding and wrinkling translucent parchments or vellums creates white lines that are permanent.

A Note: About "acid free" Papers

"Acid free" is a non-technical term that suggests that a material is permanent, durable, or chemically stable and can, therefore, be used safely for preservation purposes. The phrase is questionable, as no standards exist for acid free materials. In chemistry, "acid free" denotes a material that has a pH of 7.0 or higher. (The pH scale runs from 0 to 14. Seven is pH neutral; numbers below 7 indicate increasing acidity with 1 being the most acid. On the other side of the scale, 14 is the most alkaline.) Many vellum and parchment papers used in the projects in this book were labeled "acid free" and are, therefore, considered safe to use for memory crafting. When papers have a strong resin smell, their archival durability is questionable. ❏

Transferring Images to Parchment and Vellum

• Photocopying and Printing •
• Traditional Pen and Ink Tracing •
• Modern Pen Tracing •
• White Pencil Tracing •
• White Pencil Crayon •
• Embossing •

Photocopying and Printing

Many printers and photocopy shops have translucent vellums and opaque parchment papers in stock, and you can have your original artwork and treasured photographs copied onto these fine surfaces. Color-copied photos on translucent vellum are especially interesting. Color photocopies can be expensive, so "ganging-up" with your originals is a good idea. Place as many photographs or items as possible on a letter or legal size piece of paper. Adhere them with double-sided tape and photocopy them as one. Remove the tape immediately after the copies have been made.

You can also use an inkjet printer to print on parchment and vellum. Use a 40 lb. paper for best results. Some manufacturers have developed parchment and vellum papers especially for photocopiers and inkjet printers. Ask at your local print shop for the best paper for your use.

Traditional Parchment Lace Tracing

Traditionally, for the parchment lace technique, tracing designs on parchment is done with a mapping (split nib) pen and white ink, which complements satiny white pressure embossing for lace-like designs. Patterns can also be traced with

black, colored, or metallic inks for a variety of effects. The final success of your project depends on how neatly you trace the design.

The Steps:
1. Tape the parchment on the pattern. Because the paper is transparent, the design is very easy to see.
2. Shake the bottle of ink vigorously – opaque white inks come with a small mixing marble in the bottle to help ensure the pigment is well suspended.
3. Start tracing the design in the upper left hand corner and work down the

design to prevent your hand from smearing the image. (If you're left-handed, you'll start on the right.)

• Aim for a thin, even line – if you press too hard on the nib, it will release too much ink and the line will be too thick.

• When a pen is new, it takes a bit to get it going; parchment craft enthusiasts insist saliva is the best conditioner for a nib.

• The ink tends to collect on the nib and, even with careful cleaning, the nib will need to be replaced frequently to ensure thin lines. Always keep spare nibs around so you can change them as needed.

• Don't overload the pen with ink. Overloading can result in large drops of ink on the paper that can ruin the design.

4. Let the ink dry – it only takes a few minutes and leaves a bright, opaque image.

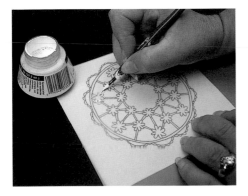

Modern Pen Tracing

Gel Pens - Until very recently, the only way to get a white design traced on parchment was with a mapping pen and bottle ink. Now that gel pens, including opaque white ones, are available, it is possible to use a continuous flow pen for tracing. However, not all gel pens work on parchment. Most gel pens have a 0.4 nib and tend to skip, making it difficult to draw a continuous line. You need a pen that has a 0.7 nib for tracing. Take the time to find one. Gel pens with colored and metallic inks work well for tracing

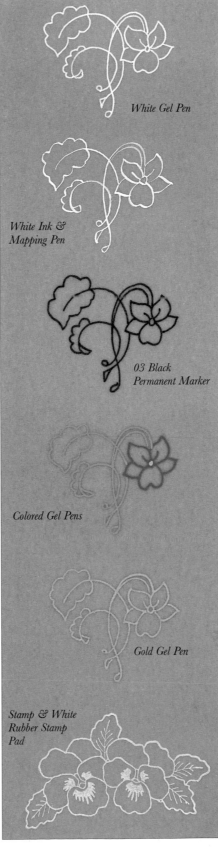

White Gel Pen

White Ink & Mapping Pen

03 Black Permanent Marker

Colored Gel Pens

Gold Gel Pen

Stamp & White Rubber Stamp Pad

designs in color, for coloring designs, and for writing messages on cards.

Black Pens - Technical pens and disposable technical pens are useful for tracing designs in black. Black-inked motifs work well with colored designs. A nib size of .03 is the best choice for a traced black line.

White Pencil Crayon Tracing

A white pencil crayon is used for drawing guidelines, borders, and fold lines on a design. It's also useful for tracing guidelines for cutting straight lines with decorative edge scissors. White pencil crayon markings are easily erased with a clean white plastic eraser.

Embossing

A unique quality of parchment paper is that when pressed with a hard point, the paper stretches and turns white. (This is the basic technique for creating raised, satiny white, shaded designs.) Many of my students prefer to trace designs with a small embossing tool rather than pen and ink.

The Steps:

1. Make a reverse photocopy of the pattern before tracing because you are working on the back side of the paper.

2. Tape the parchment on the pattern right side down. Place on an embossing pad.

3. Trace the design with the embossing tool to create a raised, white outline of the design.

Rubber Stamping

There are so many designs available today in rubber stamps that they are excellent to use as designs from parchment lace crafting or other parchment crafts. Use a waterproof inkpad with white ink and simply stamp the design onto your parchment. The design can then be embossed, pierced, or colored. For more about stamping, see "Rubber Stamping" section on page 28. ❑

Gluing, Piecing, and Laminating

- Double-sided Tape •
- Double-sided Adhesive Film •
- Laminating Film •
- Silicone-based Glues •
- Hot Glue •
- Spray Adhesives •

Using the right adhesive is vital. The most endearing quality of parchment and vellum papers – their translucency – is also the most frustrating because all glues show through the papers.

Double-sided Tape

Double-sided tapes are used to connect seams of luminaries or lampshades, to join seams to make packages, to create envelopes, and to attach folded pieces of vellum to cards. The tape is also useful for attaching photographs or other papers, as glue sticks and white craft glue do not adhere well to the smooth surfaces of parchment and vellum. Double sided tape is available in 1/4" and 1/2" widths. It will show, so cut it neatly and carefully.

Double-sided Adhesive Film

This product, (also called mounting adhesive) has backing paper on both sides. Because the film completely covers an area, the results are invisible. The sticky film adds no moisture (as some glues do) so the paper won't wrinkle or warp. You also can use a slide cutter to custom cut thin strips of double-sided adhesive to create your own double-sided tape that's the exact width you need. The film is repositionable on parchment and vellum until it is pressed down. (That technique is called "burnishing.")

The Steps:

1. Peel away the backing paper and apply the sticky side of the adhesive to the

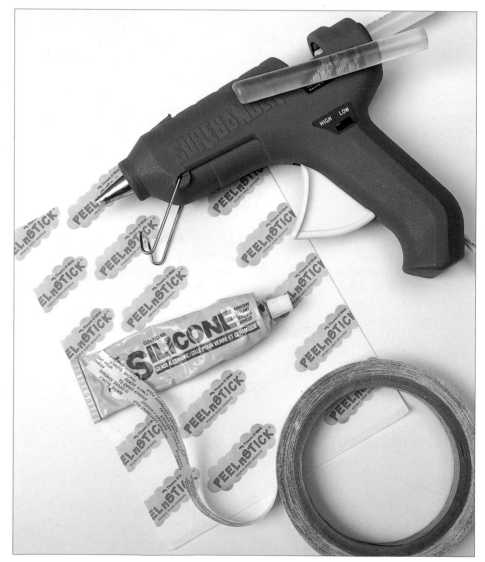

Leaves and pressed flowers that have been adhered to vellum with laminating film.

moved. Silicone glues are best for fine three-dimensional work and for adhering metal charms to papers.

Hot Glue

Hot glue (glue sticks and a glue gun) is much quicker to use than the silicone glue; the pieces stick together immediately. This makes hot glue a good choice for piecing together ornaments and three-dimensional work. This method, however, leaves no room for re-positioning or removal if you make a mistake. Use crystal clear sticks – they can't be seen under translucent papers. A "low-temperature" glue gun is best – the glue will tend to stay clear and not turn yellow or "burn" like it can with a higher temperature glue gun. Low-temperature glue is suitable for joining pieces together.

Spray Adhesive

Spray adhesive works well for laminating large pieces of paper together as well as for adhering opaque objects to vellum. Have a separate area for spraying the piece and protect the surrounding area well. Spray adhesive is very sticky and can be messy to work with.

Other Methods

Other methods for holding things together include ribbons threaded through punched holes and tied into a bow, gold threads sewn through the pieces with decorative stitches, paper fasteners, and photo corners. ❏

wrong side of the motif or trimming you wish to adhere.
2. Cut your motif or trim to size.
3. Peel away the other backing paper and position. Press in place.
 • If the backing paper is difficult to remove, slit 1/2" from the edge with the tip of your scissors for easy lifting.
 • If your cutter blade or scissors get gummed up with the sticky film, clean them with nail polish remover.

Laminating Film

Laminating film is a clear, flexible adhesive film that is sticky on one side. Simply peel away the backing paper and apply. It is used to laminate pressed flowers, feathers, and paper images to parchment and vellum. It is available in large sheets or small panels and the finishes range from shiny to matte. The matte finish is most successful on vellum papers. You also can use clear shipping labels for smaller laminating jobs.

Silicone Glue

Silicone-based glues create a strong bond that remains flexible when dry. Silicone glue can be used successfully to adhere parchment and vellum papers to each other. (White craft glues just wrinkle the paper and do not adhere well.) Silicone glue is transparent and becomes tacky in 15 to 20 minutes but does not completely dry for 24 hours. During the set time, pieces can be repositioned or

Cutting

• Craft Knife •
• Paper Trimmers •
• Craft Scissors •
• Decorative Edge Scissors •
• Cutting Mat •
• Ruler •

Sharp craft knives or paper trimmers are used to cut parchment and vellum papers to size for projects. Scissors won't give you straight, sharp edges. Make sure you have a supply of additional blades for your cutting tools to ensure you'll always have a sharp cutting edge.

Art Knife

A scalpel-type craft knife or art knife with a replaceable pointed blade is essential. It is an all-purpose cutting knife.

Paper Trimmer

A paper trimmer with a sliding blade makes cutting much easier and faster. A paper trimmer is excellent for cutting precise strips for paper weaving and for creating your own double-sided tape from double-sided adhesive sheets. You can find them in office supply catalogs and crafts stores.

Scissors

Sharp **craft scissors** are needed for cutting small pieces, decorative treatments such as ribbons, and labels. Small sharp scissors are also used for cutting out images for three-dimensional effects.

Decorative-edged scissors are available in a wide range of edge styles to give just the right finishing touch or creative edge. They can also be used to create lacy cutouts on pleated items such as fans and candle shades.

Cutting Mat

A **self-healing cutting mat** with a printed grid protects your work surface and aids accurate cutting. The mat's

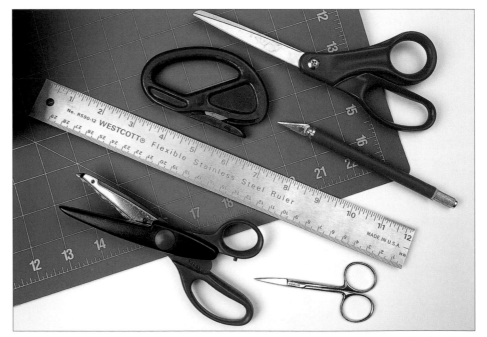

surface seals itself after each cut, so your knife won't follow a previous cut. The mats with 1", 1/2" and 1/4" grid marks make measuring and cutting perfectly square corners a breeze. The cutting mats range in size from 9" x 12" to mats that will cover an entire tabletop. Buy the biggest mat your budget will allow.

Ruler

A straight-edge **metal ruler** with a cork backing is needed for perfectly straight cuts. Wooden and plastic rulers will slide and your knife will cut into them. A selection of lengths from 12" to 18" long are useful.

Cutting Techniques

Cutting is an important skill when working with paper, and many people cut incorrectly. Here are some tips:
• Parchment and vellum papers are slicker and will slide more easily than other papers, so practice is important.

- Always measure twice and cut once.
- Use the grid markings on your cutting mat for measuring and lining up the paper. That way, you won't need to mark your paper, and your corners will be perfectly square. The transparency of the papers makes this easy.
- The key to successful cutting with a craft knife is a sharp blade. Always have extra blades handy to keep the knife in top cutting form. It is safer to use a sharp blade than a dull blade – a dull one can easily slip.
- Hold the art knife like a pen, with your index finger (it's your strongest) on top.

You make cleaner cuts by exerting a downward pressure on the blade while cutting.
- Make sure the blade is held at a constant, low angle to the paper. Make strong, one-motion cuts towards you. If you press too hard, you will drag and rip the paper.
- When cutting with your metal ruler, hold the ruler down firmly with your non-cutting hand, and keep that hand on the ruler until you've completed the cut. Keep fingers well back on the ruler and away from the blade to avoid accidents. ❏

ℱolding

• Bone Folder •
• Ruler •
• Cutting Mat •

Folding paper is a simple technique, and clean, crisp folds often determine the success of the project. Folding gives your projects strength and a sculptured look. The folds catch the light and the shadows add to the depth of the design. Lightweight vellums can be creased and folded easily; heavier parchments require scoring for a crisp fold.

The best known technique for folding paper is the accordion fold – paper is folded back and forth, somewhat like the bellows of the musical instrument. More complicated origami folds can produce interesting effects.

1. Score

2. Fold.

Bone Folder

A bone folder, which is formed from bone, is used to fold sharp creases, score fold lines, and help smooth and burnish papers. The bone does not bruise or scratch the parchment as plastic folders tend to do. An 8" bone folder with a pointed end is convenient for general work.

The Steps:

1. Because the paper is translucent, you can place it directly on the cutting mat and follow the grid lines for straight folds.
2. Place a ruler on top of parchment along the straight grid liner of mat.
3. For each fold, draw the bone folder along the ruler edge towards you, pressing down to emboss a fold line.
4. Fold along this embossed line.
5. Use the bone folder to firmly reinforce each fold by smoothing the fold down sharply. ❏

3. Press.

Coloring Parchment

• Oil Crayons •
• Stamp Pad Inks •
• Felt-tip Markers •
• Colored Inks •

There are a wide variety of colored vellums available, but you can also color your own papers. This allows you to create a mottled, antique parchment or a blended rainbow effect. Coloring techniques also include tinting small areas of motifs for a soft colored finish.

Oil Pastels & Crayons

Oil Crayons can be used to tint full sheets of paper or accent small motifs. This method is done on the **back** of the parchment after tracing on the front. Use artist's quality pastels for best results. Regular crayons do not have the required amount of pigment, and they contain a filler that can scratch and mar parchment surfaces. After you color the parchment with oil crayons, you can pressure emboss on the back and achieve a white line.

Dorso Crayons are a brand of high-quality wax crayons that were developed for the Pergamano method of parchment lace crafting. "Dorso" means "back" in Spanish, so the coloring is always done on the **back** of the parchment after the tracing has been done on the front. This technique is called "dorsing." They are heavily pigmented with no fillers.

The Steps:
1. Tape the parchment to a clean hard workspace, right side down.
2. Color the area with the crayons in even, broad strokes. *Tips:* Warm the crayon with a hair dryer before you start to help the color spread better.
3. Spread the color and soften the crayon marks. To do this, first fold a soft facial tissue into a small, firm pad. Apply a few drops of fragrance oil on the tissue pad and spread the color by rubbing vigorously until the color has spread evenly. (This also lightly perfumes your paper.) *Tip:* If the color spills over the pattern lines, use a white plastic eraser to clean up the overflow.

1. Color back of paper.

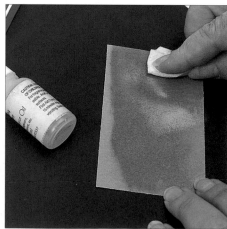

2. Spread color with oil and tissue.

3. Photo shows front of piece with the embossed lines done after the coloring.

Rubber Stamp Ink

The **ink from rubber stamp pads** can be used to stipple soft, mottled colors for an antique look. Use a waterproof dye stamp pad and a soft stippling brush.

The Steps:

1. Trace or rubber stamp an image on the parchment.
2. Pounce the brush onto the surface of the ink pad to load the brush with color.
3. Stipple the color evenly on the parchment – you can work on the front or the back. Create drifts of color on the paper for a natural, mottled look.

Markers

Water soluble **felt-tip markers** can be used to add brighter tints to small areas of your design. Use good quality markers – inexpensive children's markers do not contain enough pigment and will fade away in a matter of weeks.

This technique can be done on the front or the back of the parchment after tracing the design. Felt markers are generally worked on the front when black or colored inks have been used and on the back when white ink has been used. If you use felt markers on the front with white ink, they will color the inked lines – some-

thing you don't want. Working the colors on the back gives a softer, more muted effect.

With felt markers, you also need a #3 round paintbrush, a container with fresh clean water, and a clean cellulose sponge.

The Steps:

This method gives you a very nice shaded effect that is very easy.

1. Working one small area at a time, color the motif with a single line around the outline of the motif.
2. Dip the paintbrush in water. Remove the excess by touching the tip to the sponge – the brush should be just moist.
3. With small strokes, blend the color into the area to soften.

• Clean the brush between colors and blot on the sponge.
• If you apply too much water, the parchment will wrinkle.

1. Color the design around the outline with a marker.

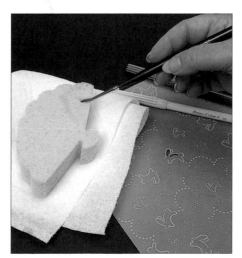

2. Blot brush on a sponge.

3. Blend color with brush.

Colored Inks

Colored inks can be used to trace your design or to paint in larger areas of a design. Work on the front of the parchment after the tracing is complete. Applied in thin layers, they produce bright, vivid colors. My favorite inks are the pearlized ones – they give a beautiful shimmer to the finished piece. Pearlized inks are easy for beginners to use.

You will need your inks, a #3 round brush, a container with clean water, and a clean cellulose sponge.

The Steps:

1. Shake pearlized inks well before starting to suspend the pigment throughout the liquid.
2. Use a very little bit of ink on your moist brush and touch the tip to the sponge to remove the excess.
3. Apply the color in even strokes.
4. Allow the ink to dry before adding another layer of color if you wish a more intense color.

Other Coloring Products

Other products that can be used to color parchment include **watercolor pencils** (either dry or wet) and **acrylic enamel paints**. ❏

Examples of Colored Designs

Felt Markers Used on Front of Parchment

Felt Markers Used on Back of Parchment

Oil Crayons Used on Back of Parchment

Pearlized Inks Painted on Front of Parchment

Pressure Embossing

* Embossing Tools *
* Embossing Pad *
* Filtered White Beeswax *
* Single Hole Piercer *
* Embossing Wheel *

Pressure embossing (also called "dry embossing") is the act of raising the surface of the parchment paper with a tool so the paper fibers are stretched and compressed by the pressure of the tool and the paper turns white.
When embossing, lighter pressure produces a soft white tone; heavier pressure produces a brighter white. Many of the lace designs in this book are simply variations of this single technique. Pressure embossing is a technique that is associated with parchment lace crafting or Pergamano.

Tools & Supplies

You must use a **heavyweight parchment** for embossing. **Pressure embossing tools** range from a very fine point to a broad shading tool – all with different effects. Pressure embossing is done on the **back** of the parchment and **after** the traced design and color (if using) are applied. All embossing must be done on an **embossing pad.** (A computer mouse pad is a good substitute.) Stippling is an embossing technique that produces a matte, dotted finish

The Steps:

1. Transfer the design to your parchment using pen and ink, a gel pen, or with a stamp using white waterproof stamp ink.
2. Place parchment piece face down on embossing pad.
3. Rub a little wax on the back of the parchment to make the embossing easier. Use only uncolored wax, preferably filtered white beeswax.
4. Use the embossing tool of your choice to emboss the design. Start with a light pressure and gently stretch the paper. Apply a little more pressure to achieve an even, white area. If you apply too much pressure, you will break through the parchment and make a hole. Build up the pressure slowly and evenly for best results.

- Use the right tool – a fine embosser to create thin lines or a spoon-shaped embosser for a large shaded embossed area.
- If the result of your embossing isn't as even or white as you'd like, use a white pencil crayon on the back of the area.
- Make sure your embossing goes right up to the traced line. If you don't, there will be a fine, dark space between the traced line and the embossed area that will detract from the overall design.

1. Transfer design.

2. Emboss larger areas.

3. Emboss details.

Embossing Examples & Tools

The examples, *right*, show different effects made by various embossing tools.

Fine Embosser - for tracing thin, white embossed lines and filling in motifs with lines.

Small Embosser - for a slightly thicker embossed white line and small dots on the design.

Medium Embosser - for filling in small areas with solid white embossing and for making dots on your design. The medium embosser is the best tool for tracing embossed lines.

Large Embosser - for large solid areas. (You can also use the rounded bottom of the medium embosser to help emboss large areas.)

Spoon-shaped Embosser - or "Hockey Stick," for making a soft, graduated shaded effect in large areas of your design. It is the main tool I use for white on white lace designs. Place the tip of the tool toward the traced outline of your design. Emboss with the pressure at the tip of the tool to create the shaded effect towards the center of the motif. Turn the parchment around as you work so the motif is always in the right position.

Single-Hole Piercer - for creating many miniature embossed dots. Stipple on the back of the parchment with the paper on a thin piece of cardboard, pouncing up and down. The piercer does not go through to the paper; it creates a minuscule embossed dot rather than a hole. You can lightly emboss an area before stippling with the large embosser to make the area even whiter. Use the stippling method for creating curly lines of small dots to accent designs.

Embossing Wheel - for creating a stippled effect similar to the effect created with the single-hole piercer that takes only a fraction of the time. I use the embossing wheel to create soft, dotted, curled lines from the motifs. The embossing wheel also allows you to stipple large areas very quickly. You will, however, need to use the single-hole piercer to fill in tight areas the wheel cannot reach and to add the final

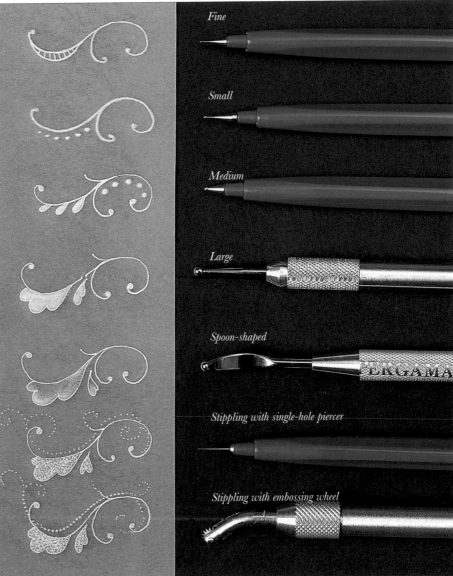

Fine

Small

Medium

Large

Spoon-shaped

Stippling with single-hole piercer

Stippling with embossing wheel

curl to stippled accent lines. (The wheel will not turn a tight corner.) Use the embossing wheel on the back of the parchment on a thin cardboard pad.

Other Embossing Tools

You can use any dry embossing tool or stylus for embossing. An embosser with three interchangeable sizes (small, medium, and large) is available where parchment crafting tools are sold and in fine art stores. You can find the spoon-shaped embosser where paper tole supplies are sold.

Piercing

• Piercing Tools •
• Piercing Pad •
• Filtered White Beeswax •

Piercing is combined with pressure embossing in the parchment lace crafting technique (Pergamano).
*Parchment piercing is done differently from paper pricking – the piercing is done from the **front** of the parchment*
and finer needles are used. The tools specifically manufactured for parchment piercing range from a single-hole piercer
right up to a eight-hole semi-circle piercer. Most piercing techniques can (theoretically) be done with a single-hole
piercer; the multi-piercing tools just make the job faster and more precise.

The Steps:

1. Tape the photocopied pattern to be pierced on the back of the parchment. Place on a piercing pad. Place the piercing pad on a cutting mat to protect your work surface.
2. Lubricate the needle for smooth piercing by rubbing the point in a piece of white wax.
3. Following the design, push the piercer all the way into the paper until it hits bottom, then pull back out with a straight up motion. Hold the needle straight, perpendicular to the paper, for perfectly formed holes.

1. Prepare parchment by placing it on a piercing pad.

2. Lubricate needle in wax.

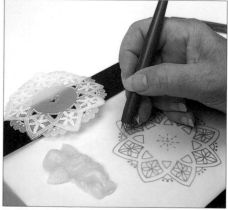

3. Pierce design.

The Piercing Tools

Single-hole piercer - A single-hole piercer is used to pierce simple designs. It can also be used for very fine embossing. The embossing is done on the back of the parchment and is a good way to add fine lines (such as veins in a leaf) or cross-hatching to a design. It can also be used to do stippling in the embossing procedure.

Two-hole piercer - This tool is mainly used for perforating an edge. This is the finishing technique that gives paper a lace-like edge. It is important that the perforations are close together and the tool has been pierced right to the bottom. After perforating, you can separate or punch out the design using your fingernail or a four-hole line tool. Improper piercing will create rips in your design. The two-hole piercer also can be used as an embosser on the back of the parchment to create an embossed cable border design. Draw a light line with a white pencil crayon on the back as a guide.

Three-hole piercer - This works well for a shaded pierced effect. The first piercing – closest to the traced line – is pushed in the whole way. The second piercing is a bit shallower, and the third is just a very light touch. The three-hole piercer also can be used to create an open pierced design with the pierce-and-wiggle technique. Pierce the parchment and, before pulling the piercing tool out, give it a little wiggle to create the design. This is very effective when done over an embossed dot.

Four-hole piercer - Designs made with a four-hole piercer are the hallmark of lacy parchment craft designs. Un-cut four hole piercing is a decorative addition to many designs.

Four-hole line piercer - This tool is very handy for perforating a lacy edge and makes a much finer edge than the two-hole piercer. Simply place the tool along the traced edge and pierce. It is also very useful when separating perforations if you are unable to use your fingernail successfully.

Five-hole piercer - This can be used to create a pierce-and-wiggle design. It also can be used to quickly pierce an even lattice pattern.

Flower piercer - This tool has seven needles in the shape of a flower. It is the only tool you do not want to push in the whole way – if you do, the middle piece will fall out, forming a large hole.

Semi-circle piercer - This tool can quickly pierce an evenly spaced scalloped or circle design. It is also used for perforating out a scalloped edge.

Examples

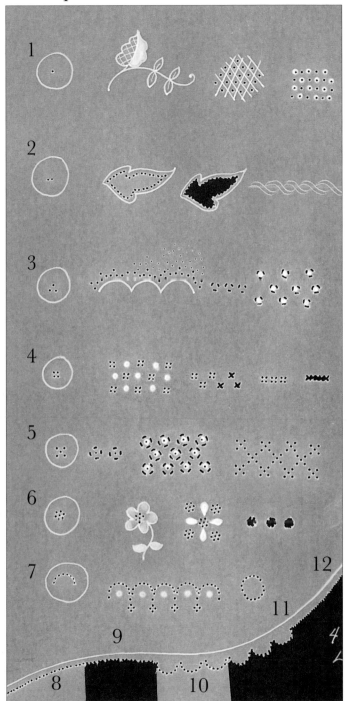

1. Single hole piercer 2. Two-hole piercer 3. Three-hole piercer
4. Four-hole piercer 5. Five-hole piercer 6. Flower piercer
7. Semi-circle piercer 8. Perforating with a piercer 9. Perforated line pushed out
10. Line edged with Semi-circle piercer 11. Perforated line pushed out
12. Line pierced and pushed out with 4-hole line piercer

Paper Pricking
• Piercing Tools •
• Piercing Pad •
• Filtered White Beeswax •

*Paper pricking is done on the **back** of a design to create a hole with a tiny embossed rim that catches the light and makes the pattern more interesting. Elaborate designs can be wrought on parchment paper to produce detailed, lacy effects.*

The craft of paper pricking is as old as paper itself – it began with the invention of paper in the emperor's court in China, where elaborate pin-pricked designs on paper were used for sacred ceremonies. By 1700, with a greater variety of papers available, paper pricking had become established as a craft. While in prison, Marie Antoinette is said to have sent a paper-pricked card to a friend. Paper pricking was a popular parlor craft during the Victorian era, when beautiful ornate papers were produced with piercing, embossing, stippling, and cutwork. The work included intricate enhanced monograms and romantic verses. This book includes simple pierced designs. You can find a large variety of patterns and books on the more detailed piercing and cutting techniques where parchment crafting supplies are sold.

Tools & Supplies

You will need a **single-hole piercer** and a **piercing pad** (a computer mouse pad or a piece of 1/2" thick foam core) along with a photocopy of your pattern. (Since you pierce the pattern as well as the parchment to create the design, always work with a photocopy.)

You can easily construct a **home-made piercer** by gluing a sharp needle into a handle made from a cork or a length of wooden dowel. I trim the needle with wire cutters to make it shorter. Insert the needle in the cork and secure with white craft glue. *Caution: Always wear eye protective goggles when cutting a needle with wire cutters – the end piece flies as it is cut.*

It is very difficult (if not impossible) to do paper pricking with a needle, unless the needle is in a handle.

Heavier parchment paper is best for paper pricking – it holds the pierced holes very well. You can also use **heavy card stock**, but be aware that the embossed edges of the holes tend to flatten out when the card is placed in an envelope.

Paper Pricking Kits are available with designs printed directly on the paper. You simply follow the design with the piercing tool, trim with scissors, and mount with double-sided tape to the front of the enclosed folded card.

Paper pricking metal templates are also available to create pricked designs. To use, tape the template to the

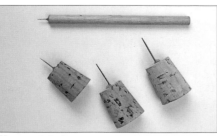

Home-made tools

back of your parchment and pierce through the evenly spaced perforations in the template. Ink a design or tape a printed image to the blank panel in the middle of the design to finish your piece before mounting on a folded card.

The Steps:

1. Tape your pattern to the back side of the parchment. Place on the piercing pad. Place the piercing pad on your cutting mat to protect your working surface.
2. Lubricate the needle for smooth piercing by rubbing the point in a piece of white wax.
3. Following the design, push the piercer all the way into the paper until it hits bottom, then pull back out with a straight up motion. Hold the needle straight, perpendicular to the paper, for perfectly formed holes. Try to achieve a rhythm that will give evenly spaced holes no closer than 1/8" apart.

Decorating with Pressed Flowers and Leaves

• Flowers and Plants •
• Flower Press •
• Laminating Film •
• Craft Scissors •

Pressing Your Own Flowers

The pressing of plants is a simple process that results in a two-dimensional product suitable for decorative use. You can use a bought flower press or a large book for pressing flowers and leaves. Pressing plants takes, on average, three to four weeks. Different plants have different drying times. You can also find a wide variety of professionally pressed flowers and leaves at craft outlets.

A partial list of flowers suitable for pressing includes hydrangea, pansy, forget-me-not, lobelia, all types of ferns, all types of leaves, leaves and flowers of herbs, larkspur, Queen Anne's lace, violets, wild roses, and sweet alyssum. Press plants as soon as possible after harvesting to prevent wilting.

The Steps:

1. Harvest the plants in the morning after the dew has dried. Collect flowers in various stages of blooming as well as the leaves and the buds of the plant.
2. Place the plants between two absorbent, smooth paper sheets (I like to use rice paper) in the press or in the book. Do not use paper towels – they will impart a pattern on the pressed plants.
3. Check the press in about two weeks. You cannot harm the process if you leave the plants in the press after they have dried, but you can damage them if you take them out before the drying process is complete.
4. Store the pressed plants flat in labeled envelopes.

Pressed Flower Stickers

Beautiful floral stickers can be made ahead and kept until you need to accent a letter, a package, or a card.

The Steps:

1. Cut out a piece of laminating film large enough to hold the floral arrangement you wish to create.
2. Peel off the backing paper and place the laminating film on your work surface, sticky side up.
3. Arrange the pressed flowers on the sticky film, placing them right side down. Position the largest blossoms first, then add smaller flowers and filler pieces. Finally, add the greenery.

• Remember you are building up your design from front to back, so the pieces put down first will be in the front of the arrangement.
• You can check the appearance of the arrangement by picking up the film and peeking underneath.
4. Place another piece of laminating film on top of the first, non-sticky side down, with the backing paper on top. Rub and press to secure.
5. Cut out the arrangement, leaving 1/8" around the edges.

To use: Peel away the remaining backing paper. Place on your project.

Variations:

• *To use only one layer of laminating film:* Rather than using a second piece of laminating film, trim around the arrangement and place on your project.
• *To make leaf tags:* Place a leaf on the laminating film, then on a piece of colored vellum. Trim the tag, leaving 1/8" all around the leaf shape. Use a permanent black marker to write on your leaf tag.
• *Try other items:* This technique also can be used with pressed fall leaves, postage stamps, punched out motifs, or feathers. ❑

Rubber Stamping
• Waterproof Dye Ink Pad • Stamps •

The range of motifs available in rubber stamps is huge; whatever motif or theme you are looking for, there's probably a stamp available! The stamps are available in tiny sizes that can be repeated to create a design, or in large sizes for instant coverage.

Supplies

The best **stamps** for parchment are simple ones without lots of shading or details. I generally use a **waterproof dye ink pad** for stamping on parchment and vellum. Some inks will not dry completely on the slick surface of the papers, and some inks will bleed into the papers. Practice on a scrap piece of paper to master the skill of perfect stamping before moving to your project.

The Steps:
1. Load the stamp evenly with the ink by lightly tapping the stamp on the ink pad.
2. Press the stamp firmly on the surface without rocking the stamp.

Tips:
• Always test your ink pads before starting a project.
• If you find some colors bleeding into the paper and creating a soft, smudged image rather than a sharp, clean-lined image, dry the ink immediately after stamping with a heat gun to prevent migration of the ink. (This practice also prevents your accidentally smudging the image before it is fully dry.)
• Choose a raised pad – it can be used with any size stamp.
• For a traditional parchment look with rubber stamps, use a white ink pad or emboss with white thermal embossing powder.

Rubber Stamp Thermal Embossing
• Embossing Heat Tool • Ink Pad • Rubber Stamps • Embossing Powders •

__Thermal embossing__ is a technique used to raise the stamped image above the surface of the paper for a dimensional effect. Many embossing powders are available – shiny, matte, glitter, and iridescent, in many different colors. Parchment and vellum paper thermal emboss beautifully.

Supplies

For this process you need a **rubber stamp, a pigment ink pad, embossing powder, and an embossing heat tool** or other heat source, such as an iron or toaster oven. (Embossing powder melts at 350 degrees F., so a hair dryer will **not** work.)

The Steps:
1. Stamp your image on the paper with pigment ink.
2. While the ink is still wet, sprinkle embossing powder on the image, completely covering it.
3. Shake off the excess powder. Place the excess powder back in the jar for later use.
4. Turn on your embossing heat tool. Blow hot air on the stamped image for a few seconds. You will see the powder melt. Do not overheat. *If you are using an iron or a toaster oven, hold the image over the heat source until the powder melts. Be careful not to scorch your paper.* ❑

Cards and Sentiments

A handmade card is a lovely gesture that will likely be a treasured keepsake. In this section, I have included examples of embossed and lace craft cards, vellum cards decorated with paper collages and charms, decoratively stitched vellum cards, rubber stamped and thermal embossed cards, pricked cards, photo cards, and cards with woven and torn paper vellum panels. The lace-like designs use basic techniques that don't require intricate cutting.

Pictured left to right: *Lace Craft Border (instructions on page 31), Quilt Lace Craft Card (instructions on page 30).*

Quilt Lace Craft Card

This card design is a sampler of simple pierced and embossed fields. The numbered illustration corresponds with the section numbers in the instructions.

Supplies

Paper

Parchment, 5" x 7"

Window card with 4" x 6" opening

Colored vellum panel

Tools and Other Supplies

White ink

Gold ink

Embossers - spoon-shaped, medium, small

Piercers - single-hole, two-hole,
    three-hole, five-hole, flower

Single-hole piercer **or** embossing wheel

Double-sided tape

Instructions

Tracing

On the front of the parchment:

1. Trace all the lines and details with white ink except the needle in the center panel, which should be traced with gold ink.
2. *Optional:* If you wish to add a saying or greeting to the center panel, pencil in the lettering with the white pencil crayon. Use white ink to add the letters.

Embossing

On the back of the parchment, on an embossing pad:

1. Use the spoon shaped embosser for the large flower in section 4.
2. With the medium embosser, emboss all the flowers in section 4 and all the small motifs and dots in sections 2, 3, 4, 5, 6, and 8.
3. With the small embosser, emboss the lines and the dots in sections 1 and 3 and the gold needle in the center panel.
4. With the two-hole piercer, emboss the double line pattern in section 7.

Stippling

On the back of the parchment, on a piece of thin cardboard:

With the single-hole piercer or the embossing wheel, add the stippled design to sections 4 and 5 and the lines in section 7.

Piercing

On the front of the parchment, on a piercing pad:

1. With the single-hole piercer, pierce the centers of the flowers in section 4.
2. With the three-hole piercer, add the pierced design to section 3 and the pierce-and-wiggle technique to sections 2 and 6.
3. With the five-hole piercer, add the pierce-and-wiggle technique to sections 6 and 8.
4. With the flower piercer, add the pierced design to section 1.

Finishing

1. Place the finished piece on the colored vellum panel in the window card. Adhere with double-sided tape. ❏

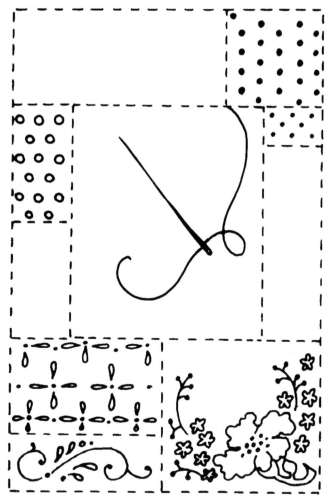

Actual Size
Pattern for
Quilt Lace Card

Lace Craft Border Card

This card includes a lace craft panel over a printed vellum panel. Both layers reveal a piece of colored card stock.

Supplies

Paper
Parchment, 8-1/2" x 11"
Colored card stock, 7-1/4" x 11"
Printed vellum, 8-1/2" x 11"

Tools and Other Supplies
White ink
Embossers - spoon-shaped, large, medium, fine
Single-hole embosser *or* embossing wheel
Piercers - flower, three-hole, two-hole
Decorative edge scissors
Double-sided tape

Instructions

Tracing
On the front of the parchment:
Trace all lines with white ink.

Embossing
On the back of the parchment, on an embossing pad:
1. With the spoon-shaped embosser, emboss all the large shapes and the flower petals.
2. With the large embosser, emboss all the larger circles.
3. With the medium embosser, emboss all the dots on the design.
4. With the fine embosser, emboss the details in the flower petals.

Stippling
On the back of the parchment, on a piece of thin cardboard:
With the single-hole piercer or the embossing wheel, add the stippled design at the center of the long motif, the veins in all the leaves, and the details in the large blossom.

Piercing
On the front of the parchment, on a piercing pad:
1. With the three-hole piercer, add a shaded pierced design to the top of the motif and the inside of the design.
2. With the flower piercer, pierce all the centers of the flowers.

Perforating
Pierce along the bottom of the motif to perforate. Separate.

Finishing
1. Fold the colored card in half. Trim the bottom edge with decorative edge scissors.
2. Fold the printed vellum piece in half. Fold the parchment piece in half. Place the vellum piece inside the parchment piece. Trim the edge of the vellum piece along the edge of the parchment piece with decorative edge scissors.
3. Assemble all the pieces. Adhere with double-sided tape at the back. ❏

Actual Size
Pattern for Lace Craft Border Card

Border & Sentiment Notecards

Patterns on page 34

These lace borders are a good project for novices. The designs can be used for cards or votive candle collars. The candle collars are pictured in the "Lamps & Luminaries" chapter.

Supplies
Paper
Parchment, 5" x 8"
Colored card stock, 5" x 8"

Tools and Other Supplies
White ink
White pencil crayon
Embossers - spoon-shaped, medium
Piercers - two-hole, single-hole
Double-sided tape

Instructions
Tracing
On the front of the parchment:
1. With a white pencil crayon, mark a 1-1/4" x 3" rectangle on the front of the card for the sentiment to be written inside.
2. Trace design with white ink, including the writing of the sentiment with white ink.

Embossing
On the back of the parchment, on an embossing pad:
1. Using the spooned shaped embosser, emboss all the larger flower blossoms and leaves.
2. With the medium embosser, emboss all the smaller shapes.
3. With the two-hole piercer, add a cable border to the traced pencil line rectangle.

Stippling
On the back of the parchment, on a piece of thin cardboard:
With the single-hole piercer or the embossing wheel, add a stippled design to the leaves.

Piercing
On the front of the parchment, on a piercing pad:
With the single-hole piercer, add some simple pierced designs to the flower centers.

Perforating
Pierce the edge of the cards in a decorative scallop or along the design edge to perforate. Separate.

Finishing
1. Fold the colored card and parchment pieces in half.
2. Attach parchment on the back with a piece of double-sided tape. ❏

Wild Rose Lace Craft Card

Patterns on page 34

An embossed and perforated parchment piece is folded around a colored paper panel.

Supplies
Paper
Parchment, 5" x 8"
Colored paper panel, 5" x 8"
Printed vellum, 5" x 8"

Tools and Other Supplies
White ink
Embossers - spoon-shaped, large, fine
Piercers - single-hole
Single-hole piercer *or* embossing wheel
Decorative edge scissors

Instructions
Tracing
On the front of the parchment:
Trace all lines with white ink.

Embossing
On the back of the parchment, on an embossing pad:
1. Using the spoon-shaped embosser, emboss the large petals, the middle shape in the buds, and half of the leaf shapes.
2. With the large embosser, emboss the stems, the tips of the buds, the small leaves, the dots in the flower center, and the border around the petals.
3. With the fine embosser, emboss the cross-hatched design in the leaf shapes.

Stippling
On the back of the parchment, on a piece of thin cardboard:
With the single-hole piercer or the embossing wheel, add the stippled veins to the flower petals and the flower buds.

Wild Rose (cont.)

Perforating

1. Draw a white pencil line across the middle of the parchment piece, but not through the design.

2. Pierce along the edge of the design that is above the pencil line.

3. Fold card along the penciled line. This will cause the perforated area to separate and extend over the folded line.

Finishing

1. Fold the printed vellum and the colored cardpiece in half.

2. Trim along the bottoms of the printed vellum and parchment piece with decorative edge scissors, using photo as a guide.

3. Assemble all the folded pieces together and attach with double-sided tape at the back. ❏

Pattern for Border & Sentiment Notecards

Thinking of You

Happy Birthday

Seasons Greetings

Thank You

Welcome

Congratulations

Actual Size Patterns
for Wild Rose
Lace Craft Card

Actual Size Patterns for Lace Craft Window Cards

Lace Craft Window Cards

This trio of lace designs is an easy project for a beginner. Only simple embossing and tracing techniques are used. Different colors of vellum are placed behind the embossed designs.

Supplies

Paper
Parchment, 3" x 3" for each card
Window card with envelope
Brightly colored vellum, 4" x 5-1/2",
 to back the finished design

Tools and Other Supplies
White ink
Embossers - spoon-shaped, large,
 medium, fine
Embossing wheel **or** single-hole piercer
Double-sided tape

Instructions

Tracing
On the front of the parchment piece:
Trace all lines with white ink

Embossing
On the back of the parchment, on an embossing pad:
1. With the spoon-shaped embosser, emboss the outer flower petals and the flower buds.
2. With the large embosser, emboss the flower stems and half of the leaf motifs.
3. With the fine embosser, emboss a cross hatch design in the other half of the leaf motifs and the small lines on the stems and buds.
4. With the medium embosser, add the dots to the inside of the flower.

Stippling
On the back of the parchment, on a piece of thin cardboard:
With the embossing wheel or the single-hole piercer, stipple the design on the flower petals and in the flower buds.

Finishing
Use double-sided tape to adhere the finished parchment piece in the window card in front of a piece of colored vellum.
❑

Charmed Vellum Cards

All of these cards are made with colored and patterned vellums and small metal charms, using the same simple layering technique. For best results, choose a charm that coordinates with the patterned vellum.

Supplies

Colored vellum *or* card stock
Patterned vellum
Scraps of handmade paper
Charms or other embellishments

Instructions

1. Cut a piece of colored vellum or card stock to 4-1/2" x 8-1/2". Fold in half. (This forms the inner card.)
2. Cut the patterned vellum pieces to the same size. Fold in half. (This forms the outer card.)
3. Glue the inner card to the vellum piece with a 5" piece of double-sided tape on the back of the card.
4. Accent the cards with torn pieces of handmade paper, pieces of ribbon, and dried leaves. Apply with spray adhesive.
5. Pieces of decoratively cut vellum are adhered on top of the paper or ribbon. First place the vellum on double-sided adhesive film. Use decorative edge scissors or a slide cutter to cut the accent shape. Peel off the backing paper and adhere to the card.
6. Adhere charms, bows, or tassels with silicone glue. ❑

Floral Bouquet Embossed Card

Supplies

Paper
Parchment, 5-1/2" x 7"
Mauve card stock, 4-1/2" x 6-1/4" with
   a 3" x 4" oval window
Gray card stock, 7" x 11"

Tools and Other Supplies
White ink
White pencil crayon
Oil pastels
Spoon-shaped embosser
Single-hole piercer **or** embossing wheel
Double-sided tape

Instructions

Tracing
On the front of the parchment:
1. Trace all lines with white ink.
2. With a white pencil crayon, mark along the dotted lines. (The white inked saying was added after the card was mounted in the front panel.)

Coloring
On the back of the parchment:
With oil pastels, color all the flowers and leaves.

Embossing
On the back of the parchment, on an embossing pad:
Using the spoon-shaped embosser, emboss all the flowers and leaves.

Stippling
On the back of the parchment, on a piece of thin cardboard:
With the single-hole piercer or the embossing wheel, add the stippled veins on the rose leaves.

Cutting
With scissors, cut out along the floral edge in between the penciled line.

Finishing
1. Mount the finished parchment piece behind the cut oval with the floral bouquet on the outside of the panel.
2. Attach the piece to the panel with double-sided tape.

Actual
Size
Pattern

3. Attach the parchment piece and panel to the folded card with double-sided tape.
4. Add a saying, a dotted ink design, and a line border with white ink to accent the card. ❏

Decoratively Stitched Vellum Cards

On these cards, a vellum panel creates a transparent veil over a decorative motif. The motifs are outlined with decorative stitching, which is done with gold thread. The cards fit nicely in vellum envelopes, 5-3/4" x 4-3/8".

Supplies

Paper

Colored card stock, 5-1/2" x 8-1/2",

Colored card stock, 5-1/2" x 4-1/4" (for the inside panel)

Plain vellum, 5-1/2" x 4-1/4" (for the covering panel)

A decorative motif from an old greeting card or color photocopy of an antique card (Maximum size should be 4-1/2" x 3".)

Instructions

1. Score down the middle of the 5-1/2" x 8-1/2" card stock for the fold.
2. With double-sided tape, adhere the decorative motif to the front of the card.
3. Place the vellum panel on the front of the folded card. Hold in place while piercing the holes for the decorative stitches.
4. Thread a needle with gold metallic embroidery floss. Attach the vellum panel with decorative stitches. Do not knot the thread on the back; tape down the ends of the threads.
5. Adhere the smaller piece of card stock to the inside of the card to hide the stitches and tape. ❑

Lily of the Valley Embossed Card

Pictured on page 41

See the Basic Techniques section for instructions on coloring with ink.

Supplies

Paper

Parchment, 7-1/2" x 11"

Colored card stock, 7-1/2" x 11"

Tools and Other Supplies

White ink

Pearlized inks - emerald green, white, yellow green

Embossers - fine, spoon-shaped, small, medium

Single-hole piercer **or** embossing wheel

Five-hole piercer

Decorative edge scissors

Double-sided tape

Instructions

Tracing

On the front of the parchment:

1. Ink the stems and leaves with emerald green pearlized ink.
2. Ink the flowers and sentiments with white ink.
3. Write a sentiment with white ink.

Coloring

On the front of the parchment:

Continued on next page

Lily of the Valley (cont.)

1. Paint the leaves with yellow green pearlized ink.
2. Paint the flowers with white pearlized ink.

Embossing

On the back of the parchment, on an embossing pad:

1. Using the spoon-shaped embosser, emboss all the leaves and flowers.
2. With the small embosser, emboss the lettering. Emboss all the dots on the border design.
3. With the two-hole piercer, emboss the design in the border.
4. Add the border line details with a fine embosser.

Stippling

On the back of the parchment, on a piece of thin cardboard: With the single-hole piercer or the embossing wheel, add the stippled design leaves and flowers.

Piercing

On the front of the parchment, on a piercing pad: Using the five-hole piercer and the pierce-and-wiggle technique, pierce around the embossed dots in the border design.

Finishing

1. Score and fold the colored card.
2. Score and fold the embossed parchment piece.
3. Trim the edges of the parchment with decorative edge scissors.
4. Place the parchment over the card stock. Adhere the parchment on the back of the card with double-sided tape. ❑

Pattern for Lily of the Valley
Enlarge @182% for Actual Size

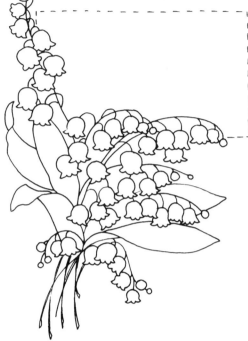

Violet Posy Embossed Card

Supplies

Paper

Rainbow parchment, 4" x 6"
Window card with envelope

Tools and Other Supplies

White ink
Felt markers
Embossers - spoon-shaped, medium
Single-hole piercer **or** embossing wheel
Double-sided tape

Actual Size Pattern for Violet Posy

Instructions

Tracing

On the front of the parchment:

Trace all lines with white ink.

Coloring

On the back of the parchment:

With felt markers, color the design.

Embossing

On the back of the parchment, on an embossing pad:

1. Using the spoon-shaped embosser, emboss the flowers, leaves, and stems.
2. With the medium embosser, emboss the small leaves and dots.

Stippling

On the back of the parchment, on a piece of thin cardboard:

With the single-hole piercer or the embossing wheel, add the curled stippled design to the bouquet.

Finishing

Adhere the finished piece and the backing panel to the inside of the card with double-sided tape. ❑

Pattern for Bluebell
Enlarge @155% for Actual Size

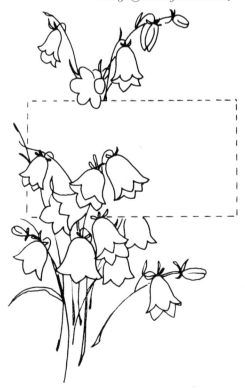

Bluebell Embossed Card

See the Basic Techniques section for instructions on coloring with ink.

Supplies

Paper
Parchment, 7" x 10"
Colored card stock, 7" x 10"

Tools and Other Supplies
White ink
Pearlized inks - green, blue
White pencil crayon
Embossers - spoon-shaped, fine, small
Single-hole piercer **or** embossing wheel
Decorative-edge scissors
Double-sided tape

Instructions

Tracing
On the front of the parchment:
1. Ink the stems and leaves with green pearlized ink.
2. Ink the bluebells with blue pearlized ink.
3. Ink the sentiment with white ink.
4. Trace the dotted line with a white pencil crayon as a guide for the border placement.

Coloring
On the front of the parchment:
Paint the bluebells with blue pearlized ink.

Embossing
On the back of the parchment, on an embossing pad:
1. Using the spoon-shaped embosser, emboss all the bluebells.
2. With the small embosser, emboss all the stems and leaves and the lettering. Emboss all the dots on the border design.
3. With the fine embosser and a ruler, emboss a double line for the border. Add the border line details.

Stippling
On the back of the parchment, on a piece of thin

Pictured left to right: *Lily of the Valley Embossed Card, Bluebell Embossed Card, Violet Posy Embossed Card*

cardboard:
With the single-hole piercer or the embossing wheel, add the stippled design to the bluebell flowers.

Finishing
1. Score and fold the colored card.
2. Score and fold the embossed parchment piece.
3. Trim the edges of the parchment with decorative edge scissors.
4. Place the parchment over the card stock. Adhere the parchment on the back of the card with double-sided tape. ❑

Rubber Stamped Cards

These cards began with images that were rubber stamped on colored vellum for a variety of effects. The stamped image panels were adhered with double-sided adhesive film on the fronts of the cards. Cord, tassels, additional stamped and thermal embossed images, charms, and photo corners were added for decorative effects. The size of the card is determined by the size of the rubber stamps.

Pictured clockwise from top right: *Three Graces, Pagoda, Goldfish, Stargazer*

Project Descriptions

Three Graces - The image is stamped in green ink, mounted on a panel to make a border, and adhered to a green card with thermal embossed gold leaves. A panel mounted on the inside creates a border for the front of the card. Gold cord is threaded through punched holes and tied in a bow.

Pagoda - Image is stamped in black ink on a red panel, mounted on a gold panel, and adhered to a card. A Chinese character is thermal embossed in gold on the envelope and a scrap of black card stock. The card stock character is cut out and mounted with a dimensional dot. A red tassel is threaded through punched holes.

Goldfish - The image is stamped in black on metallic vellum and thermal embossed, then cut out and mounted on a vellum panel. A cutout window on the card front is bordered with thermal embossing. The vellum panel is glued behind the window.

Stargazer - The image is stamped in dark blue on blue vellum, cut out, and mounted on a black patterned vellum pattern with silver photo corners. A silver-leaf star is applied to the image. The panel is trimmed to fit the front of the card.

Evergreen - Leaves are rubber stamped on the front of the card with green ink. The main image is stamped in black on printed vellum and mounted on a light green vellum panel with a decorative edge. The panel is adhered to the front of the card and trimmed with preserved cedar and a bow.

Amor - The "Amor" rubber stamp creates a tone-on-tone background and a panel that's decorated with a postage stamp and a golden bird charm on this card composed of two layers of card stock. The locket is a heart-shaped piece of printed vellum mounted on a gold vellum cutout with a "ribbon" cut from the same gold vellum.

Mother and Child - The layered card is off white card stock with a cover of gold vellum. The image is stamped in black and trimmed to create a narrow border, then mounted on a deep red vellum panel. Printed sheer ribbon and a gold and copper leafed fleur de lis decorate the front.

Floral Border - A vertical stamped floral border and vellum pieces cut with decorative edge scissors trim this card. The image of a woman's face is stamped on gold vellum. A thermal embossed fleur de lis completes the card. ❑

Pictured clockwise from top right:
Evergreen, Amor, Mother and Child, Floral Border

*Pictured left to right, standing: Purple
Pansies, Tulip, Nosegay, Purple Rose.*
*Pictured left to right, lying down: Blue
Pansies, Lacy Heart.*

Floral Window Cards

   *In this collection of cards, the images are stamped on parchment panels with
white ink and thermal embossed with white embossing powder. Different techniques
were used to color and accent the cards.*
   *The panels were placed in purchased pre-made window cards and backed with a
colored or printed vellum panel to finish. The two pansy cards were made with the
same stamp, but the finishing techniques yield decidedly different results.*

Project Descriptions

Purple Pansies - Colored with felt markers on front of panel, cutout bordered with line of green metallic ink.

Tulip - Pierced and stippled, flower perforated, rainbow panel placed behind parchment, cutout bordered with line of white ink.

Nosegay - Colored with felt markers, cutout bordered with line of green metallic ink.

Purple Rose - Colored with felt markers, backing panel stamped with "Thank You" stamp.

Blue Pansies - Colored with oil crayons, sentiment written with metallic ink around cutout.

Lacy Heart - Stamped and thermal embossed on printed parchment, dotted border added with white ink. ❏

Snowflake Card Collection

This collection of cards shows the different variations you can achieve using one rubber stamp with purchased window cards. See Basic Techniques section for information on various techniques used.

Pictured at left (clockwise from top right):
White Sparkles - *Thermal embossed with white sparkle powder on snowflake-printed vellum, colored with felt markers; small snowflakes stamped and thermal embossed with white sparkle powder on card*

Golden Rainbow - *Thermal embossed in gold on rainbow vellum, colored with gold ink; decorative punch and metallic ink dots on card*

Welcome Winter - *Thermal embossed in gold on rainbow vellum, colored with inks, glitter paint, perforated; inked greeting on card*

Pictured at right (left to right):
Pink Snowflakes - *Thermal embossed in white on pink vellum, colored with inks, stippled, pierced border; decorative punch and paper pricking on card*

Joy - *Thermal embossed in silver on pale blue vellum, colored with inks, perforated, pierced, stippled, backed with green vellum; sentiment added in silver ink as a border on card*

Actual Size
Patterns for Angel Card Panels

You're
an Angel

Angels live
among us

Thank heaven
for you

Believe
in
Miracles

Angel Card Panels

These designs can be mounted in window cards or matted to create prints suitable for framing. The designs were all worked the same way. The sizes of the mats are proportional to the sizes of the designs.

Supplies

Paper
Parchment, 7" x 8"
Cream opaque parchment paper, 6" x 7-1/2"
Tan parchment card stock, 6-1/2" x 8"

Tools and Other Supplies
Inks - black, red, green, blue, gold
White pencil crayon
Pearlized inks - blue, green, red
Felt markers - yellow, beige, white, rose
Embossers - spoon-shaped, large, medium, fine
Single-hole piercer **or** embossing wheel
Decorative edge scissors

Instructions

Tracing
On the front of the parchment:
1. Trace the angel and lettering with black ink.
2. Trace the roses with red ink.
3. Trace the leaves with green ink.
4. Trace the forget-me-nots with blue ink.
5. Trace the border with a white pencil crayon.

Coloring
On the front of the parchment:
1. With felt markers, color in the angel.
2. With pearlized inks, fill in the floral garland.

Embossing
On the back of the parchment, on an embossing pad:
1. Using the spoon-shaped embosser, emboss the angel.
2. With the large embosser, emboss the angel's wings and the roses.
3. With the medium embosser, emboss the leaves, flowers, and the dots on the border design.
4. With the fine embosser, add the decorative border.

Stippling
On the back of the parchment, on a piece of thin cardboard:
With the single-hole piercer or the embossing wheel, add the stippled design to the floral garland.

Finishing
1. Mount the finished piece on tan parchment card stock. Trim edges of card stock with decorative edge scissors.
2. Frame the design with a mat cut from cream parchment paper.
3. Outline the mat opening with gold ink.❏

PAPER PRICKED CARDS

Paper pricked cards can be created from patterns, with paper pricking templates, or with paper pricking kits. See the Basic Techniques section for information about each technique. On the pages that follow, examples of each variety are pictured.

Actual Size Pattern for Oval Panel Pricked Card

Actual Size
Pattern for Fuchsia
Pricked Card

48

Fuchsia Pricked Card

Pictured on page 50.

This simple, elegant greeting card has a delicately pierced fuchsia growing along the edge.

Instructions:

1. Tape the pattern on the far left side of a sheet of heavy parchment and pierce the design.
2. Cut along the outside edge of the motif.
3. Fold the paper in half.
4. Fold the dark purple vellum liner in half. Place in the card and adhere with double-sided tape.
5. Add a greeting to the front of the card with a rubber stamp or hand write with a purple gel pen. ❏

Oval Panel Pricked Card

Pictured on page 50.

This parchment card is a beautiful frame for an image cut from a recycled greeting card (as shown here), a rubber stamped design, or a photocopy of a photograph.

Instructions:

1. Score and fold an 8-1/2" x 11" sheet of heavyweight parchment in half.
2. Hold the pattern to the front while you cut the outer edge with scalloped edge scissors.
3. Open up the paper and tape the pattern to the left hand pane, lining up the scalloped edge.
4. Pierce the design. Remove the pattern.
5. Fold the card.
6. Adhere the image to the oval panel in the front. ❏

Violet Bouquet Pricked Card

Pictured on page 51

Instructions:

1. Create a pricked parchment design using a metal template of your choice and heavyweight parchment.
2. Trace the pattern from the "Violets Posy Embossed Card" on page 40 in the center of the panel with black ink.
3. Color the design with felt markers.
4. Adhere the panel to the front of a green card. ❏

Glove Pricked Card

Pictured on page 51.

This card was inspired by a popular 17th century verse ("If that from GLOVE, you take the letter G, then GLOVE is LOVE and that I send to thee") and the old-time tradition of giving gloves to a sweetheart.

Instructions:

1. Tape the pattern to a sheet of heavyweight parchment paper.
2. Pierce the design.
3. Score along the dotted line.
4. Cut out on the solid lines. Shape.
5. Write the verse inside the card. ❏

Actual Size Pattern

With
Best
Wishes on
Your
Birthday

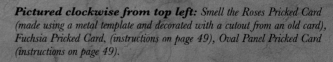

Pictured clockwise from top left: *Smell the Roses Pricked Card (made using a metal template and decorated with a cutout from an old card), Fuchsia Pricked Card, (instructions on page 49), Oval Panel Pricked Card (instructions on page 49).*

Pictured clockwise from top right: *Blackberry Pricked Card (made from a paper pricking kit), Violets Bouquet Pricked Card (instructions below), Glove Pricked Card (instructions on page 49), Fairy Pricked Card (made from a paper pricking kit).*

51

Photo Accordion Card

This charming display card holds six favorite photographs for a charming memory gift. The vellum overlays on the photographs help to soften and blend the photos so the overall look is consistent even if the photos are very different pictures.

The frame for the card is a 30" x 5" strip of heavy card stock folded accordion style into 5" square panels. The photographs and vellum panels were trimmed to 3-1/2" square and are held to the card with white photo corners. Decorate the front of the card with a hand-lettered title on a panel attached with photo corners to a printed panel. ❏

Celebrate
the
little
things

Photo Greeting Cards

These cards are a great way to create a simple, personalized greeting that's sure to become a keepsake. Enclose the cards in vellum envelopes.

Instructions

1. Cut a 5-1/2" x 8-1/2" piece of a dark colored card stock. Cut a vellum piece with a small printed pattern the same size.

2. Score each piece to make a card 4-1/4" x 5-1/2". Fold.

3. Adhere a photocopy of a favorite family photograph to the front panel of the card with double-sided tape.

4. Attach the vellum piece to the outside of the card with a 5" piece of double-sided tape on the back.

5. Finish your card by adding a border with a greeting or salutation around the photograph with a permanent pen. ❑

Woven Parchment Cards

Weaving with translucent vellums creates interesting patterns that are aesthetically pleasing on a card, as a bookmark, or as a luminary panel. For weaving, cut the vellum into 1/2" or 1/4" wide strips with a slide trimmer. Weaving is a great way to use up all those thin strips of paper left over from other projects.

I especially like to weave rainbow parchment papers – the results are stunning. You can create your own rainbow parchment with oil pastels.

Instructions

1. Carefully line up half of the parchment strips on your work surface and tape one side to hold.
2. Weave all the remaining strips through the taped down strips.
3. Carefully hold down the woven piece while lifting off the tape.
4. Adjust the piece as needed. Place a laminating sheet on top of the piece.
5. Peel away from the surface and adhere to the backing paper specified.

To Make Cards:

1. Create a square or rectangular woven panel to fit your chosen card size.
2. Cut a piece of double-sided adhesive film the size of the woven area, **not** including the loose ends. (This leaves the ends sticking out for an interesting effect.)
3. Using double-sided film, adhere the woven panel to the card or to a coordinating piece of rainbow vellum.
4. If you used a vellum panel, add a border with a gold gel pen.

To Make Bookmarks:

1. Create a woven panel 1-1/2" to 2" wide and 5" to 6" long.
2. Laminate the woven piece, using a piece of clear crafting plastic.
3. Trim to size.
4. Install a metal eyelet about 3/8" from the edge of one short side.
5. Thread a tassel through the eyelet.

To Make Luminaries:

1. Create a woven panel or panels.
2. Insert in a luminary frame. See the Lamps, Luminaries, and Lanterns section for instructions on making luminaries. ❏

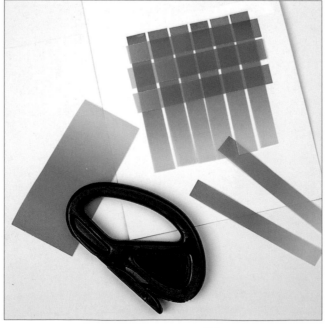

Torn Vellum Landscapes

Parchment and vellum papers are very easy to tear, and the paper has a soft white edge where torn. These torn pieces can be layered to make fantasy landscapes and seascapes for cards and luminaries – their beauty is revealed when the panels are backlit and the colors merge for a striking effect. These landscape panels were placed in windows cut from card fronts and luminaries and attached with double-sided tape. If you cut the second piece of laminating film larger than the first, you can cover the back of the panel and adhere it to its card or luminary frame at the same time.

Instructions

1. Cut two pieces laminating film, each 4-1/2" x 6".
2. Cut rainbow parchment and colored vellum into strips 3" wide and 1" to 6" long.
3. Tear the colored strips into mountain shapes, tree shapes, or any abstract shape you like.
4. Remove the backing from one piece of laminating film. Place on your work area, sticky side up. *Note: You are working from front to back, so the first piece you place on the film will be the front of your design.*
5. Arrange the torn paper pieces into fantasy seascapes and landscapes. Add dried ferns or leaves if you like.
6. When you are pleased with the arrangement, place the other piece of laminating film over the panel to form the backing.
7. Trim the panel to size. Use in a card or luminary.

Torn Landscape Luminaries

Pictured on page 57

These torn landscape luminaries are panels set in a paper card stock frame with a semi-circular stand attached on the back. The one at left uses paper pieces only; the one on the right includes small pieces of dried fern fronds that look like evergreen trees in the landscape. The openings of the recycled paper frames were accented with lines of gold ink.

To make the stand, cut a piece of matching card stock (2-1/2" x 9" for a 5-1/2" x 4-3/4" frame). Fold each short end under 1/2". Attach the folded ends to the back of the frame with double-sided tape. ❏

Lamps, Luminaries, and Lanterns

I have been making and using paper lanterns, luminaries, and candle shades for years — I love the way parchment diffuses the light and adds atmosphere to any room.

Paper lanterns and luminaries are meant to be used with glass votive candle holders. Paper candle shades can be used on wineglasses or on candle followers to create a candle lamp. Candle followers are shade holders made of brass that are designed to fit on taper candles. As the candle burns, the follower "follows" it down, and the shade moves with the light. You can also use the brass shade holders that fit in candlesticks and hold small tea lights.

Be Safe!

We used to display a paper shade on a candle follower with a burning candle in our store and let it burn for hours to show customers that the shades don't easily catch fire. Because the heat is directed straight up from the candle, the paper stays very cool. Danger can come when the candle is left unattended — when a cat could knock the shade over or a gust of wind could blow the paper into the path of the flame. **Never** *leave a lighted candle unattended.*

Pictured above: *Single Panel Luminaries. See instructions on page 64.*

Pastel Collars

These collars have two layers – an inner colored piece and an outer white one. The top edges of the colored pieces are trimmed with decorative edge scissors. The top edges of the white pieces are embossed with lacy floral borders. They are made using the same patterns and techniques as the "Lace Craft Border Cards." See page 33. The parchment is 3-1/2" x 7-1/2"; the colored vellum liner is 3" x 7-1/2".

Elegant Candle Collars

With heavyweight parchment paper and roller-type rubber stamps, it's easy to create exquisite votive candle collars. These trimmed collars are quick and inexpensive to create – fill the table with them for a striking arrangement.

Cut a parchment rectangle that, when rolled into a cylinder shape, will fit around your candleholder. Decorate by embossing, stippling with color, or adding images with rubber stamps, choosing motifs to suit your decor and the season. After decorating, form the parchment into cylinders and adhere with double-sided tape. Place the candle holders and candle collars on a low dish or other heat-proof surface to complete the effect.

Gold Embossed Collars

Load a roller stamp with thermal embossing ink and roll along the top edge of the parchment paper. Sprinkle on gold embossing powder and heat to set.

Silver Snowflake Candle Collars

Snowflakes were stamped with a roller-type rubber stamp on white parchment and thermal embossed with silver powder. Use them with clear glass or frosted votive candle holders.

Folded Candle Collars

Strips of vellum are accordion folded to create these fancy candle collars.

Instructions

1. Cut the vellum into 8-1/2" x 3" for the outside collar and 8-1/2" x 4" for the inside sleeve.
2. Fold the strips in 1/2" accordion-style folds.
3. Cut along the folds on one side of both collars with decorative edge scissors, cutting only the edge. (If you cut too deeply, the collar will be weakened by the large open space.)
4. *Optional:* Cut the tops of the collars with scissors to create scallops when unfolded.
5. Unfold.
6. *Optional:* Decorate the top edge of the inside collar with decorative hole punches.
7. Form into cylinders and secure with doubled-sided tape.
8. Place inside sleeve over the outside collar. Place over glass votive candle holders. ❑

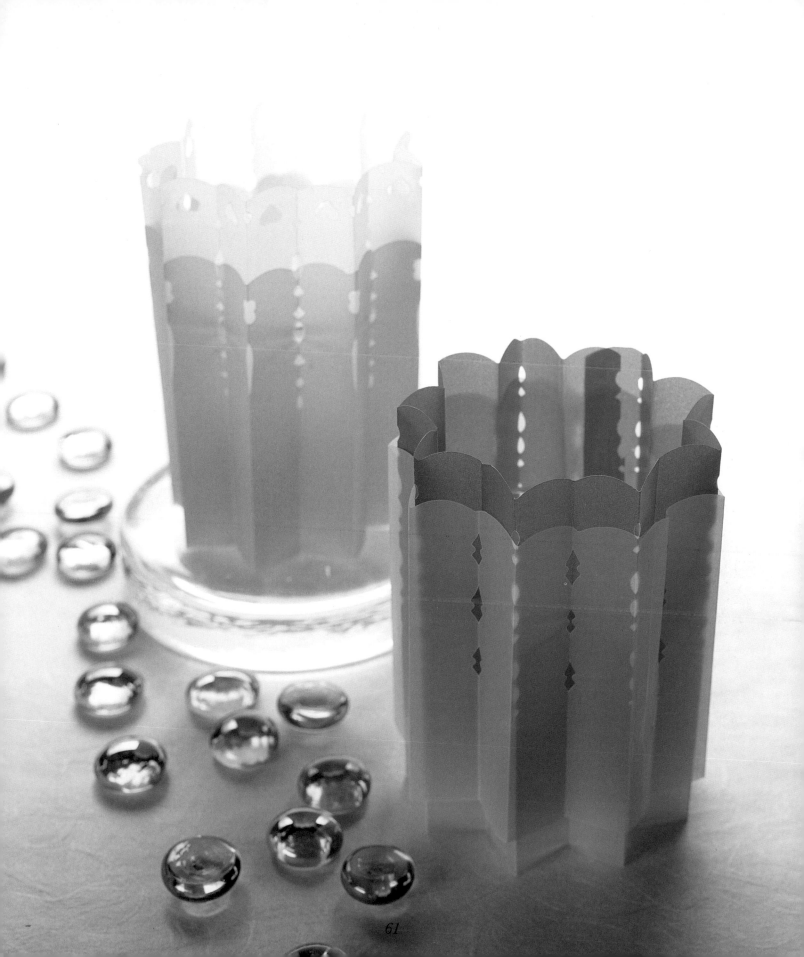

Three-Panel Luminaries

Three-panel luminaries are triangle-shaped. The frames are made of card stock with windows cut in them for the luminary panels. You can cut a window in each panel or just cut one window in the center panel. Descriptions and general instructions appear below.

Instructions

1. Cut the luminary frame from a piece of heavy card stock, 5" x 15-1/2". Score at 5" intervals to create three 5" square panels and a 1/2" seam.
2. Cut 3" square windows in the center panel or in all three panels of the frame.
3. Decorate the frame with rubber stamps, tape, or lettering.
4. Make the panel or panels and trim to 4" square. The panels can be a rubber stamped image on a piece of vellum, color photocopies on vellum, or pressed flowers, leaves, or feathers sandwiched between two pieces of vellum. Make the "sandwich" panels by adhering double-sided adhesive film to a piece of vellum. Arrange pressed flowers, skeleton leaves, or feathers on the sticky film. Place a second piece of vellum on top of the arrangement. Press to secure.
5. Adhere the panels to the inside of the frames with double-sided tape or decorative metallic tape.
6. Add extra sparkle inside panels without windows with adhesive-backed metallic papers. Cut the metallic paper into 4-1/2" squares, peel off the backing paper, and adhere to inside of frame. The metallic paper linings help reflect the flicker of the candle and add to the luminous mood.
7. Overlap the seam and join with double-sided tape.

Project Descriptions

Pictured at right, back to front:

Feathers - Cut one window. Stamp frame with feather design, using a rubber stamp. Make a panel with feathers on adhesive film and sandwich between blue vellum. Line uncut panels with silver metallic paper.

Leaves - Cut three windows. Stamp frame with leaf designs, using rubber stamps. Make three panels with skeleton leaves on adhesive film and sandwich between layers of white vellum. Attach panels inside frame with copper tape.

Dreams - Cut one window. Stamp vellum panel with rubber stamp, using black ink. Write "The future belongs to those who believe in the beauty of their dreams" around the image with silver ink. Line uncut panels with gold metallic paper.

Pansy - Cut one window. Make a pressed flower panel and sandwich between layers of off white vellum. Line uncut panels with copper metallic paper. Make a border for the cut panel with copper tape.

Vacation - Cut three windows. Photocopy three vacation photos on vellum. Write the date and place with silver ink. ❏

The future belongs to the beauty of their dreams

Strathacona Park 1998

Single-Panel Luminaries

These simple single panel luminaries are made to fit into votive candle holder frames. The panels are made with feathers, skeleton leaves, or pressed flowers that are sandwiched between layers of vellum, wrapped with copper tape, and decorated with a metal charm.

Instructions

1. Adhere double-sided adhesive film to a piece of vellum.
2. Arrange pressed flowers, skeleton leaves, or feathers on the sticky film.
3. Place a second piece of vellum on top of the arrangement and press to secure.
4. Trim the finished panel to 3" x 4".
5. Wrap the edges with copper tape. Add extra interest by cutting the edge of the tape with decorative scissors before applying to the panels.
6. Attach a charm to the front with silicone glue. ❏

WINEGLASS OR CANDLE FOLLOWER SHADES

These shades show off the luminous qualities of colored and patterned vellums. They can be used to create a lamp from a wineglass or a candle follower. Two patterns are provided – one is for a tall shade, the other for a wide shade. Choose one to fit your wineglass; either will fit a candle follower.

To use your wine glass shade, fill a wineglass half full of water and place a floating candle in it. Light the candle, using a long match, and place the shade on the rim of the wineglass. (If you don't have a long match, use a piece of uncooked spaghetti. It works!)

Pattern for Seashore Pricked Shade

Enlarge @118% for actual size

Seashore Pricked Shade

The seashell motif was designed to fit on the tall shade pattern.

Supplies

Paper
Ecru heavyweight parchment

Tools and Supplies
Single-hole piercer
Decorative edge scissors
Double-sided tape
Craft knife

Instructions

1. Photocopy the pricking pattern.
2. Trace the tall shade pattern on page 70 on the back of the parchment. Tape the pattern for pricking in place.
3. Prick the design.
4. Cut out the curved edges shade with decorative edge scissors.
5. Cut out the straight edges with a craft knife.
6. Form the cone shape and adhere with double-sided tape. ❑

Lace Embossed Candle Shade

Pictured on page 69

Supplies

Paper
Parchment, 9" x 12"

Tools and Other Supplies
White ink
Embossers - spoon-shaped, large, medium, fine
Single-hole piercer **or** embossing wheel

Instructions

Tracing
On the front of the parchment:
Trace all the lines and details with white ink.

Embossing
On the back of the parchment, on an embossing pad:
1. Using the spoon shaped embosser, emboss all the large motifs, leaves, and flower petals.
2. With the large embosser, emboss all the small flowers and stems.
3. With the medium embosser, emboss all dots on the design.
4. With the fine embosser, add the vein lines to the flower petals and leaves.

Stippling
On the back of the parchment, on a piece of thin cardboard:
1. With the single-hole piercer or the embossing wheel, add the stippled technique to the large flower and curled shapes.
2. Add curly lines coming from the design into the center of the shade.

Perforating and Cutting
1. Pierce the top and bottom of the shade to perforate, following the design lines.
2. Cut out the two straight sides with a craft knife.

Finishing
Adhere the short sides together with double-sided tape to form the shade. ❏

Pattern for Lace
Embossed Candle
Shade

Enlarge @ 155% for actual size

White Flowers Thermal Embossed Shade

Supplies

Paper
White parchment

**Tools and Other
   Supplies**
White pencil crayon
Rubber stamp
Pigment ink pad
White embossing powder
Piercers - flower, single-hole
Decorative edge scissors
Craft knife
Double-sided tape

Instructions

1. Trace the wide shade
   pattern from page 70 on
   white parchment with a
   white pencil crayon.
2. Rubber stamp a floral
   design and thermal
   emboss with white
   powder.
3. Pierce the centers of the
   embossed flowers.
4. Add a pierced flower-and-
   leaf design with a flower
   piercer and single-hole
   piercer.
5. Cut out curved edges with
   decorative edge scissors.
   Cut out straight edges
   with a craft knife.
6. Form into cone shape and
   adhere straight edges with
   double-sided tape. ❏

*Pictured left to right: Lace Candle Shade,
White Flowers Thermal Embossed Shade*

Candle Shade Pattern -
Wide Style

Candle Shade Pattern -
Tall Style

Enlarge patterns @118%
for actual size

Snowflake Thermal Embossed Shade

The embossed snowflake shade lined with red would be wonderful for winter holidays; this idea could be adapted to any season or theme.

Supplies

Vellum, white and red
Snowflake rubber stamps, various sizes
Embossing powder, gold
Decorative-edge scissors

Instructions

1. Using the tall shade pattern on page 70, trace the shade outline on white vellum and colored vellum with a white pencil crayon.
2. Rubber stamp motifs on the white vellum and thermal emboss with embossing powder.
3. Cut out the colored shade just outside the pattern lines, using decorative edge scissors on the curved edges and a craft knife on the straight edges.
4. Cut out the white embossed shade just inside the pattern lines, using decorative edge scissors on the curved edges and a craft knife on the straight edges. (This makes the inner shade slightly larger than the outer shade, so the colored vellum will show at the top and the bottom.)
5. Form each shade into a cone shape and adhere with double-sided tape. Place the colored shade on a prepared wineglass or candle follower and place the white embossed shade on top. (There is no need to glue the two shades together.) ❑

Lace & Purple Shades

Both shades are made with lace-patterned printed vellum and purple vellum liners. The shade at left is made with the tall pattern; the shade on the right is made with the wide pattern. Mix and match the colored liners and patterned shades for different occasions and room decor.

Supplies

Vellum, white printed and colored
Decorative-edge scissors

Instructions

1. Using the patterns on page 70, trace the shade outline on white printed vellum and colored vellum with a white pencil crayon.
2. Cut out the inner shade (the colored one) just outside the pattern lines, using decorative edge scissors on the curved edges and a craft knife on the straight edges.
3. Cut out the outer shade (the white printed one) just inside the pattern lines, using decorative edge scissors on the curved edges and a craft knife on the straight edges. (This makes the inner shade slightly larger than the outer shade, so the colored vellum will show at the top and the bottom.)
4. Form each shade into a cone shape and adhere with double-sided tape. Place the colored shade on a prepared wineglass or candle follower and place the white printed shade on top. (There is no need to glue the two shades together. ❑

Seashore Turquoise Shade

This shade uses white vellum printed with seashell motifs and the wide shade pattern. It is made in the same way as the "Lace & Purple Shades." See the instructions on page 71.

Tribal Lantern

This simple lantern, stamped with motifs similar to those found in cave paintings, is made to fit a metal candle stand. A clear glass votive candle holder and white votive are placed inside the lantern.

Supplies
Stamps in a variety of sizes and designs
Four stamp pads – green, bronze, gray, and navy
White parchment
Small natural sea sponge

Instructions
1. Determine the circumference of the candle stand and add 1/2" to the circumference measurement. Determine the height you wish the lantern to be. You can make the lantern any height you desire, depending upon the size of your stand. Draw a rectangle for your lantern measurements on parchment with white pencil crayon.
2. Sponge the various ink colors lightly on the parchment. Let dry.
3. Stamp the motifs around the paper using the various colors of ink.
4. Cut the parchment rectangle along marked lines on sides and bottom using a craft knife.
5. Carefully tear the top edge for a rustic uneven edge.
6. Roll parchment in a cylinder shape and secure with double-sided tape. Place in candle stand. ❏

Japanese Lantern

This simple lantern, made to fit a metal candle holder, is decorated with roller rubber stamps. Use a roller-type stamp with Chinese characters and lighter-colored ink to create the stripes of Chinese characters in the background. Use a bamboo design stamp with black ink to create the main motifs.

Instructions

1. Determine the circumference of the candle stand and add 1/2" to the circumference measurement. Determine the height you wish the lantern to be. You can make the lantern any height you desire, depending upon the size of your stand. Draw a rectangle for your lantern measurements on parchment with white pencil crayon.
2. Stamp the "stripes."
3. Stamp the bamboo motifs around the lamp, varying the heights.
4. Cut along the marked lines on the bottom and sides with a craft knife.
5. Cut the top edge with deckle decorative scissors.
6. Roll parchment in a cylinder shape and secure with double-sided tape. ❑

Simple Lanterns

Sometimes simple is best. These lanterns are merely plain, unadorned parchment paper cut to size, rolled into cylinders, and secured with double-sided tape.

Classical Lantern

Here the lantern started with parchment that had a crackle design finish. A variety of ink colors (mostly metallic) and rubber stamps – standard and roller-type – in classic-inspired motifs (columns, leaves, stars, a woman's face, and a clock face) are layered and overlapped. After the stamping a calligraphy message was added. This one says, "The brightest light does not come from outside but from within..."

Containers, Gifts, and Packages

Parchment and vellum can be used to make uniquely beautiful gift packaging and wraps — the translucent packages hold a soft glimpse of what's inside. In this section, you'll see how to make containers, scented sachets, tea sachets, gift tags, and envelopes.

Pictured clockwise from top right: *Cedar-Trimmed Tall Bag-Style Parcel, Small Twisted Cylinder, Feather-Stamped Three-Sided Parcel, Medium Twisted Cylinder, Large Twisted Cylinder. Instructions are on the following pages.*

Twisted Cylinders

Pictured on page 77 &79

Twisted cylinders are easy and quick to make. The size of the paper and the way you join the seams determine the size and shape – no pattern is needed. They are held together with double-sided tape and hot glue. The largest of the packages was made from a 8-1/2" x 8" rectangle of heavyweight parchment.

Instructions

1. Form a cylinder from a square or rectangular piece of paper, overlapping 1/2". Adhere the sides together with double-sided tape.
2. Double fold the bottom of the cylinder with two 1/4" folds. Adhere with hot glue. This closes the bottom of cylinder.
3. Place the gift inside through the remaining opening. Close this opening by double folding with 1/4" folds at a 90 degree angle to the first folds.
4. Secure with a gold seal or a staple. Add labels and embellishments to accent and finish the parcel. ❏

Making Embossed Labels

Pictured on page 79

I used an oval-shaped frame stamp on pale pink vellum to make these labels. A square, rectangle, or circle frame stamp also would work nicely.

Instructions

1. Stamp frame on vellum and thermal emboss the image with white sparkle embossing powder. Stamp as many as you can fit on the paper so you have lots on hand.
2. Remove the backing paper from a sheet of double-sided adhesive film. Place it on the back of the sheet of stamped images.
3. Cut out the individual labels from the sheet.
4. When you are ready to use a label, write a greeting or the contents of the parcel on it with a gel pen. Remove the backing paper and adhere the label to the parcel. ❏

Three-Sided Parcel, Tall Bag-Style Parcel, and Folded Cornucopia

Pictured on pages 77, 79, and 82

These three package types are made the same way. The three-sided parcel is a triangular box. The tall bag-style parcel is formed like a paper grocery bag – it stands on its flat bottom and is fastened at the top. The cornucopia has four long, triangle-shaped panels that meet in a point at the bottom.

These parcels are perfect containers for small handcrafted gifts, homemade and purchased candies, or fragrant potpourri. Adjust the size of the parcel by reducing or enlarging the patterns provided on a photocopier.

The parcels can be adorned with rubber stamps, floral or feather seals, leaf labels, parchment roses or dragonflies, ribbons, or raffia – see the photos of the packages for ideas. If you're using transparent paper and you wish to hide the gift, place it in a bed of crinkled paper basket filler or wood excelsior.

Instructions

1. Tape the parchment over the pattern provided. (If you are using opaque parchment, the pattern will need to be on top.) Place parchment on an embossing pad.
2. With a medium embosser or a bone folder, trace all the solid and dotted lines. Where you trace, the parchment will turn white, and you will have scored the fold lines. Remove the pattern.
3. Referring to the pattern, cut along all lines that are solid on the pattern using scissors or a craft knife.
4. *Optional:* If you wish to decorate the paper with rubber stamps, do so now while the parcel is flat.
5. Fold along the other marked lines (the dotted lines on the pattern) to form the parcel.
6. Adhere long seams with double-sided tape. Adhere short flaps with hot glue, leaving one end open to insert the gift.
7. To make it easy for the recipient to retrieve the gift without damaging the parcel, close the top with a paper fastener, a gold seal, a floral seal, or a bow made by looping ribbon through punched holes. ❏

Pattern for Tall Bag-Style Parcel
Enlarge @125% for actual size

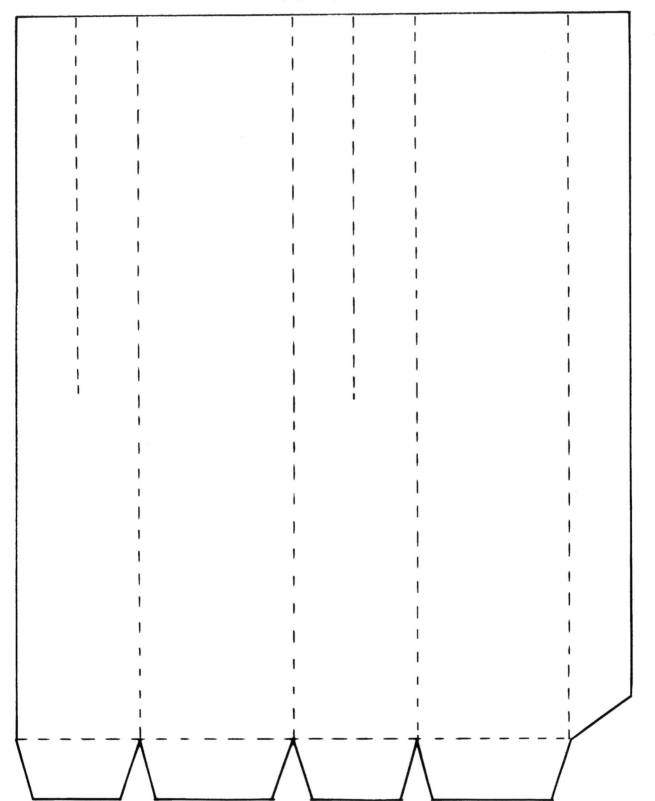

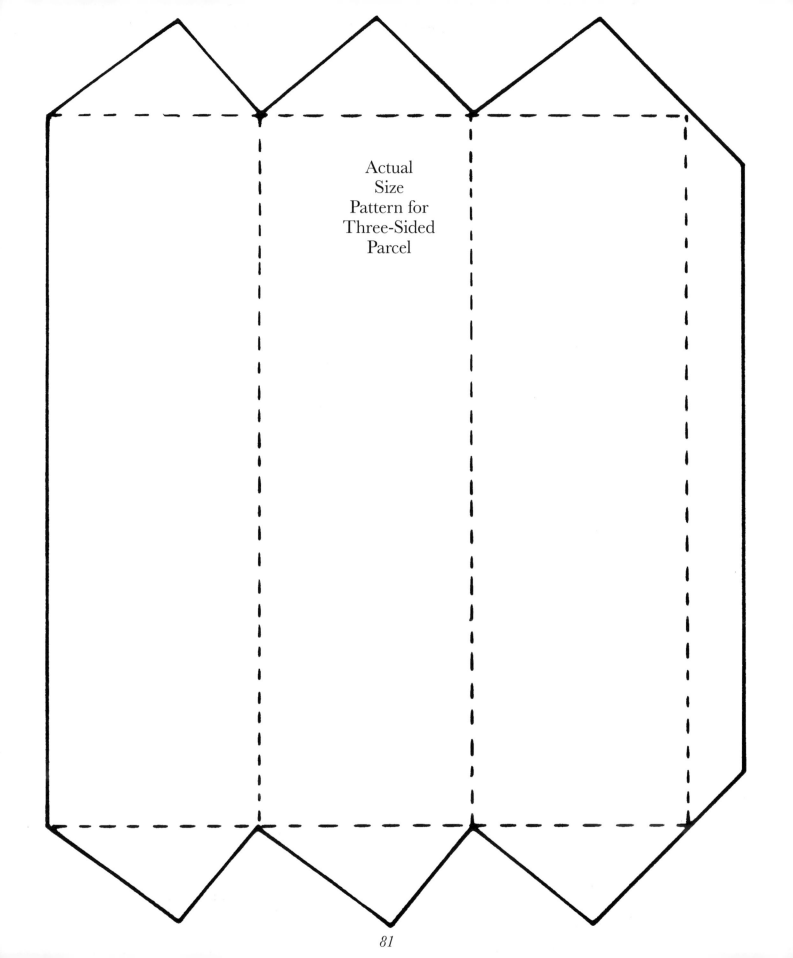

Actual
Size
Pattern for
Three-Sided
Parcel

Three Cornucopia Sachets

See page 84 for pattern. See page 78 for General Instructions.

Pictured from top:

Rainbow Cornucopia with Flowers - Cut cornucopia from rainbow vellum. Leave top open and fold flaps out. Insert flowers.

Rainbow Cornucopia with Gold Seal - Cut cornucopia from rainbow vellum. Fill with candies. Fold top flat and seal with a gold document seal.

Rosebud Cornucopia - Cut from translucent vellum. Fill with candies. Wrap with thin iridescent ribbon. Make a multi-loop bow from ribbon and glue on top. Glue a satin rosebud at the center of the bow. ❑

Lace Craft Cornucopia and Lace Craft Nosegays

Instructions on page 84, 85

Pictured top to bottom: *Small Lace Craft Nosegay, Lace Craft Cornucopia Sachet, Large Lace Craft Nosegay, Small Lace Craft Nosegay decorated with Rose and Butterfly.*

Lace Craft Cornucopia Sachet

Pictured on page 83

This cornucopia parcel is filled with fragrant, colorful potpourri and adorned with sheer ribbon, silk flowers, and a metal filigree cone. It looks complicated but takes only a short time to make. You can get two 7" cornucopias from one sheet of parchment paper.

Supplies

Paper
Translucent parchment

Tools and Other Supplies
White pencil crayon
White ink
Medium embosser
Single-hole piercer **or** embossing wheel
Double-sided tape
Glue gun and glue sticks

Trims
Sheer ribbon, 1/4" wide
Small white artificial flowers
Gold filigree cone

Instructions

Tracing
On the front of the parchment
1. Trace the outline and the fold lines of the design (the dotted lines) with a white pencil crayon.
2. Trace all the other design elements with white ink.

Embossing
On the back of the parchment, on an embossing pad:
Using the medium embosser, emboss the flowers, leaves, and dots on the pattern. Also emboss the fold lines of the parcel.

Pattern for Lace Cornucopia Sachet

Enlarge @118% for actual size

Stippling
On the back of the parchment, on a piece of thin cardboard:
1. With the single-hole piercer or the embossing wheel, add the stippled lines to the top and bottom of the design.
2. Add the curly lines from the flower motif.

Piercing and Cutting
1. Pierce the small lines at the bottom of the design to perforate. (These slits will have a piece of ribbon threaded through them.)
2. Cut out the parcel.

Finishing
1. Weave a piece of sheer ribbon through the slits. The ends of ribbon should be on the outside.
2. Assemble the cornucopia. Secure the seam with double-sided tape.
3. Fill with potpourri.
4. Fold down the top flaps and glue with a glue gun.
5. Add a sheer ribbon bow and a small bunch of silk flowers to the top of the sachet. Tie the threaded-through ribbon in a bow. Add the metal filigree cone to the pointed end. ❑

Lace Craft Nosegays

Pictured on page 83

These lacy nosegays are perfect backgrounds for a small bunch of flowers, a handmade parchment rose and butterfly, or the saved icing flowers from a wedding or anniversary cake. They make wonderful decorations for a shower or a special favor for a bridal luncheon.

Supplies

Paper
Large - 6" parchment square
Small - 4-1/2" parchment square

Tools and Other Supplies
White ink
Embossers - large, medium
Piercers - single-hole, flower, semi-circle, two-hole
Craft knife

Trims
Floral posies made with silk flowers
Sheer wide ribbon, 7/8" wide

Instructions

Tracing
On the front of the parchment:
Trace all lines with white ink.

Embossing
On the back of the parchment, on an embossing pad:
1. Emboss all large areas with the large embosser.
2. Emboss all dots with the medium embosser.

Stippling
On the back of the parchment, on a piece of thin cardboard: Large Nosegay - With the single-hole piercer or embossing wheel, add the stippled design to the large nosegay in the lined designs between the flowers.

Piercing
On the front of the parchment, on a piercing pad:
1. Small Nosegay - With the single-hole piercer, add a pierced design in and around the flowers.
   Large Nosegay - With the single-hole piercer, add the design around the dots in the border design.
2. With the flower tool, add the center to every flower.

Perforating
Large Nosegay - Pierce the edge to perforate. Separate.
Small Nosegay - Pierce the edge with the semi-circle piercer to perforate. Use the two-hole tool at the points of the design. Separate. Pierce the small fan-shaped sections and triangles to perforate and remove for an even more lacy effect.

Finishing
1. Cut a starburst in the center of the nosegay with a craft knife. Poke in the prepared posy.
2. Tie a bow with the sheer ribbon on the stems at the back of the nosegay to finish. ❏

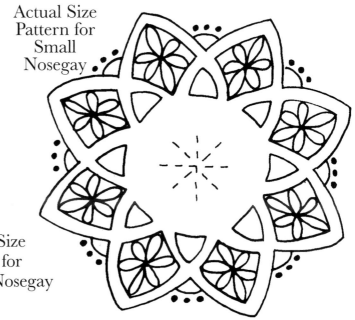

Actual Size Pattern for Small Nosegay

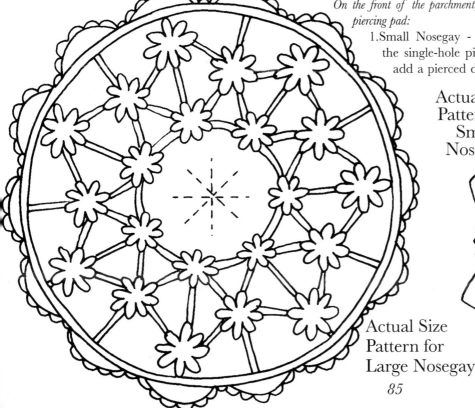

Actual Size Pattern for Large Nosegay

VELLUM ENVELOPE SACHETS

It's easy to construct envelopes that are just the right size for their contents. For a square envelope, simply enlarge or reduce the envelope pattern provided using a photocopier. For a rectangular envelope, make the pattern narrower or wider, then enlarge or reduce to size.

*The envelopes pictured on the following pages are sachets. Large or small vellum envelopes can be filled with potpourri to make lovely, fragrant drawer sachets for drawers, linen closets, suitcases, or any place that needs a fragrant refresher. The beautiful potpourri that fills them can be seen and **smelled** through the translucent package. They also make a wonderful enclosures to add to a gift of a handmade article of clothing, a crocheted blanket, or a handstitched quilt. They are so pretty you will want to keep some around for yourself.*

General Instructions for Envelope Sachets

1. If needed, enlarge envelope pattern on a copier.
2. Place parchment on top of pattern. Using a medium embosser or a bone folder, trace all the solid and dotted lines onto parchment. Where you trace, the parchment will turn white, and you will have scored the fold lines. Remove the pattern.

Continued on page 88

 Tea Bag Sachets

These tea sachets are made of colored vellum using the envelope pattern, which was sized to fit a standard single-serving tea bag. Double-sided tape is used to close the flaps. Sheer ribbon and little tea charms finish off the packages. Tea bag packages can be so lovely and the tea so aromatic that they make gorgeous little sachets to give as gifts or favors.

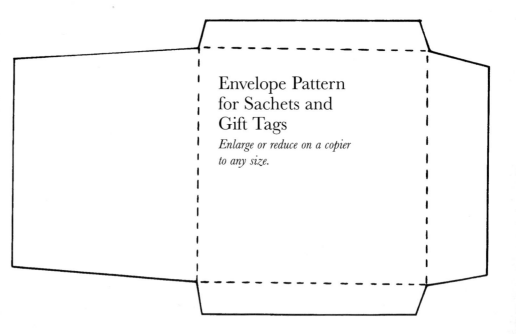

Envelope Pattern for Sachets and Gift Tags
Enlarge or reduce on a copier to any size.

Pictured from top: *Monogrammed Square Sachet, Rose Square Sachet, Floral Rectangular Sachet. The square sachets measure 8-1/2"; the rectangular sachet is 5-1/2" x 7-1/4". The two square sachets are decorated with adhesive-backed metal charms. The rectangular envelope is decorated with a pressed flower sticker. See the section "Decorating with Flowers & Leaves" in the General Techniques chapter.*

General Instructions (cont..)

3. Referring to the pattern, cut along all lines that are solid on the pattern with scissors or a craft knife.
4. Fold along the other marked lines (the dotted lines on the pattern) to form the envelope.
5. Adhere the sides with double-sided tape.
6. Place scented potpourri in the envelope. Close up the envelope, using double-sided tape all around the flap's edge. The tape successfully seals all the edges and keeps the potpourri in the envelope.
7. Decorate the sachets with floral seals, pewter self-adhesive charms, or silk flowers and leaves. ❑

Fall and Floral Sachets

The **Fall Sachets** pictured below are filled with a spicy-scented potpourri to which silk oak leaves were added. The envelopes measure 4-1/2" x 5-3/4". They are trimmed with natural raffia, silk leaves, and artificial acorns.

The **Floral Sachets** pictured on the following page feature Floral Gift Tags, a Floral Rectangular Sachet, Daisy Charms Square Sachet. The square sachet measures 8-1/2"; the rectangular sachet is 5-1/4" x 7-1/4". They were made using the envelope pattern provided.

Fragrant Blend for Scented Sachets

Use this fragrant blend for linen closets and drawers.

Mix together:
1/2 cup of finely ground lemon peel
1 tablespoon crushed coriander
1 tablespoon grated nutmeg
1 tablespoon crushed whole cloves
1/4 cup lavender buds

Add:
A few drops of lavender essential oil
Mix well. Let the blend mellow for a week before placing in a vellum envelope.
Optional: Add dried or silk flower blossoms for color and a floral look. ❑

Floral Gift Tags

These gift tags feature colorful, unique cards in envelopes made of translucent patterned vellum. The envelopes are 3" square and are made using the envelope pattern. The cards are color photocopies of garden flowers and leaves.

Instructions

1. Photocopy fresh flowers and leaves them on good quality white paper. (You can also photocopy the flowers on vellum with beautiful results.)
2. Cut out the shapes with a pair of sharp scissors.
3. Write your message with a gel pen on the back of the card.
4. Make envelope. Install a silver or brass grommet in one corner. Thread with thin ribbon. Insert the card and tuck in the flap. ❑

Capturing Nature

Pressed flowers and leaves are beautiful additions to gift bags, window panels, placecards, and greeting cards. See "Decorating with Pressed Flowers and Leaves" in the Basic Techniques chapter for information on preserving greenery from your garden and instructions for making flower stickers.

Pressed Flower Placecards

Lacy placecards are easy to make. They would be lovely for a bridal tea, a Victorian tea, or to dress up the table for a dinner party. The design can also be used for gift tags.

Supplies

Paper
For each card:
Colored vellum, 3" x 5"
Lace printed vellum, 3" x 4"

Tools and Other Supplies
Bone folder
Double-sided tape
Decorative edge scissors
Pressed flower sticker
White gel pen

Instructions

1. Score each piece of vellum in half and fold.
2. Trim the lace vellum with a pair of decorative edge scissors.
3. Adhere the lace piece to the colored piece with double-sided tape at the back.
4. Add a pressed flower sticker on the front.
5. Write the name on the card with a white gel pen. ❑

Pressed Flower Cards

These cards are made with pre-embossed vellum panels and colored card stock. The greetings can be rubber stamped or hand lettered. See the Basic Techniques section for instructions for making pressed flower stickers.

Supplies

Paper
Pre-embossed vellum panel,
   5-1/2" x 8-1/2"
Colored card stock, 5-1/2" x 8-1/2"
Vellum envelope

Tools and Other Supplies
Bone folder

Rubber stamp ("Thank You")
Stamp pad with dark ink
2 pressed flower sticker
Double-sided tape

Instructions

1. Score and fold card stock in half.
2. Score and fold vellum panel in half.
3. Rubber stamp the greeting on the front of the card stock.
4. Attach the vellum panel to the colored card stock with a 5" piece of double-sided tape at the back. *Option:* Punch two holes at the top of the card. Tie the vellum panel to the colored card with a piece of 1/4" wide sheer ribbon.
5. Attach a sticker on the front of the vellum panel.
6. Trim the card stock with decorative edge scissors.
7. Place in a vellum envelope.
8. Seal with a second flower sticker. ❏

Gift Bags with Stickers

These beautiful frosty gift bags are made of a very sturdy plastic, so they last for many gift exchanges and are even strong enough to use in the boudoir or powder room as a small, pretty trash container. Find them at card and gift shops. They coordinate wonderfully with handmade vellum and parchment cards and gift tags.

Large sheets of laminating film were used to make large floral and leaf stickers for the fronts of the bags. These bags came with cord handles, but I replaced them with sheer ribbon bows.

Framed Nature Prints

These framed pressed ferns and leaves are designed to sit in the window so they are backlit. The vellum panels – one leaf per panel, four panels per frame – give the leaves a muted, layered appearance. The instructions that follow are for the smaller 5" x 7" panels. For the large collage, use a larger frame with divided panels. Two vellum panels were made to fit frame. One panel is made with skeleton leaves and is behind the front panel that has three pressed leaves and a fern frond.

Supplies

Flat wooden frame with 5" x 7" opening
2 pieces clear glass, each 5" x 7"
6-8 pieces frosted vellum (two for each
   leaf or frond), each 5" x 7"
3-4 leaves or fern fronds
Silicon glue
White acrylic craft paint
Sponge brush
Sandpaper, medium grit

Instructions

1. Paint frames with white acrylic paint. Let dry.
2. Sand frames to achieve a weathered whitewash look.
3. Place one piece of glass in the frame.
4. Construct the vellum panels, using one leaf or frond per panel. Hold in place with a tiny drop of silicon glue.
5. Layer the vellum panels in the frame and top with the second piece of glass.
6. Secure glass in frame. ❑

Decorations, Celebrations, and Memories

Parchment and vellum make marvelous three-dimensional table decorations and ornaments for holidays and other special events. Parchment crafting techniques also can be used to create framed pictures and photo mats and albums. This section provides numerous examples.

Wild Rose Table Decorations

Lovely vellum roses accent the placecard, the candle shade, and the table. They are perfect decorations for a bridal tea or a wedding dinner and are surprisingly quick to make. A lace craft nosegay is a nice addition. See "Lace Nosegay" instructions in the Containers, Gifts, and Packages chapter.

The placecards are patterned vellum accented with a border of dots made with white pearl fabric paint. To make the lace-printed vellum shade, use the pattern for the tall shade in the Lamps, Luminaries, and Lanterns chapter. Accent the shade with dots of white pearl fabric paint, three wild roses, and extra leaves.

Wild Roses

Supplies

Paper
Rainbow vellum
Green vellum

Tools and Other Supplies
Embossing wheel
Wooden dowel
Glue gun and glue sticks
Gold dimensional fabric paint
Pearl spray

Instructions

1. Cut two wild rose petal pieces from rainbow vellum.
2. Cut one leaf from green vellum.
3. Stipple veins on each petal and leaf with the embossing wheel.
4. To create dimension, roll one petal piece around a wooden dowel.
5. With a glue gun, adhere the leaf to the center of the bottom petal piece, then add the top (dimensional) petal piece.
6. To make the flower center, apply six dots of gold fabric paint. (The fabric paint forms beautiful dimensional centers and helps hide the glue.) Let dry.
7. Spray with a light coating of pearl spray to strengthen and beautify. ❑

Pattern for Wild Rose Petals

Pattern for Wild Rose Leaf

Christmas Lace Trio

This Christmas trio includes a votive candle collar, a menu card, and a design for placecards. They are accented with three-dimensional poinsettias. The menu card records the meal. Have everyone at the table sign it. Add the date and save for a beautiful memory.

Placecard & Menu Card

Patterns on page 100

Supplies
Paper
Parchment - 4-1/2" x 5-1/4" for placecard, 8-1/2" x 4-1/2" for menu card, 4" x 8" for candle collar
Red card stock - 5" x 5-1/4" for placecard, 6" x 9" for menu card
Red vellum - 4-1/2" x 8-1/4" for candle collar

Tools and Other Supplies
White ink
Embossers - spoon-shaped, large
Single-hole piercer **or** embossing wheel
Glue gun and sticks
Three-dimensional vellum poinsettias (Instructions follow.)

Instructions
Tracing
On the front of the parchment:
Trace all the lines with white ink.

Embossing
On the back of the parchment, on an embossing pad:
1. Emboss all the large open areas with the spoon-shaped embosser.
2. With the large embosser, emboss the flower centers and the smaller flowers.

Stippling
On the back of the parchment, on a piece of thin cardboard:
1. With the single-hole piercer or the embossing wheel, stipple the leaves and stems, the veins in the large flowers, and the lines in the curled shapes.
2. On the menu card, add stippled curled lines to accent the lettering.

Perforating

Pierce the edges alongside the embossed designs. Separate.

Finishing
Place card - Fold where indicated. Add name with white ink on the vellum. Glue on the parchment poinsettia.
Menu card - Fold the card stock and parchment piece in half. Add parchment piece with a piece of double-sided tape. Glue on the parchment poinsettia.
Candle collar - Form red vellum into a cylinder and secure with double-sided tape. Form parchment into cylinder and slip over vellum. Check overlap. Secure with double-sided tape. Glue on the parchment poinsettia. ❑

Three-Dimensional Poinsettias

Patterns on page 100

Supplies
Paper
Red vellum
Green vellum

Tools and Other Supplies
Embossing wheel
Wooden dowel
Glue gun and glue sticks
Gold dimensional fabric paint
Gold glitter spray
Optional: Varnish

Instructions
1: Cut two poinsettia blossoms from red vellum.
2. Cut three leaves from green vellum.

Continued on page 100

Wire Napkin Ring and Placecard Holder

The wire placecard stands are formed with a 16" piece of green wire. (Fig. 1) The napkin ring is made with two 12" pieces of green wire twisted together in the middle for 6". (Fig. 2) Form the twisted part into a 2-1/2" diameter circle and coil the ends. (Fig. 3)

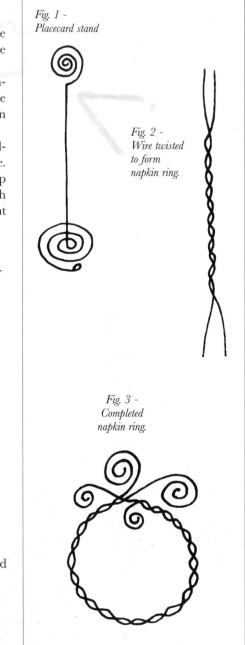

Fig. 1 - Placecard stand

Fig. 2 - Wire twisted to form napkin ring.

Fig. 3 - Completed napkin ring.

Three-Dimensional Poinsettia (cont.)

3. Stipple veins on each petal and leaf with the embossing wheel.
4. To create dimension, roll one blossom piece around a wooden dowel.
5. With a glue gun, adhere the leaves to the center of the bottom (flat) blossom piece, then add the top (dimensional) blossom piece.
6. To make the flower center, apply six dots of gold fabric paint. (The fabric paint forms beautiful dimensional centers and helps hide the glue.) Let dry.
7. Spray with a light coating of gold glitter spray. A coat of varnish can be added to strengthen and beautify. ❑

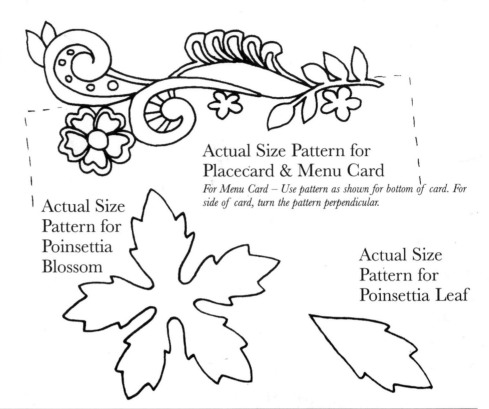

Actual Size Pattern for Placecard & Menu Card

For Menu Card – Use pattern as shown for bottom of card. For side of card, turn the pattern perpendicular.

Actual Size Pattern for Poinsettia Blossom

Actual Size Pattern for Poinsettia Leaf

Dragonfly Ornament

These whimsical critters are designed to clip on a parcel, a wine glass, or the top of an open card on display. **Do not** *use them on candle collars; if they overhang the candle, they could catch on fire.*

Supplies

Paper
Rainbow parchment
Translucent parchment

Tools and Other Supplies
Silver gel pen
Embossing wheel
Scissors **or** craft knife
7" green wire
Glue gun and glue sticks

Instructions

Tracing
1. Trace the body of the dragonfly with a silver gel pen on rainbow parchment.
2. Trace the wings with a silver gel pen on translucent parchment.

Stippling
Stipple the veins and body accents on the pieces with an embossing wheel.

Cutting
Cut out the pieces.

Finishing
1. Form the wire piece. See Fig. 1.
2. Glue the wings to the wire. Glue the body to the wings. ❑

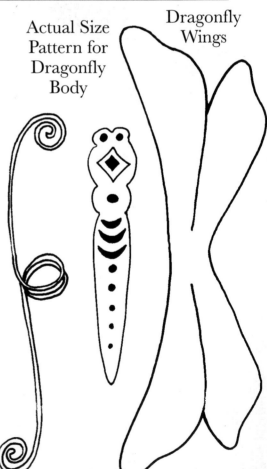

Actual Size Pattern for Dragonfly Body

Dragonfly Wings

Fig. 1 - Pattern for Shaping Wire for Dragonfly

Snowflake Bobeches

Bobeches are placed in candlesticks to catch dripping wax and decorate the candle and candlestick. To make them, I used a large snowflake stamp. (A single blossom stamp or round motif stamp would also work.) The stamp should be about 3" in diameter.

Instructions

1. Stamp the snowflake on heavy translucent parchment.
2. Thermal emboss the images with white sparkle embossing powder.
3. Cut out the shapes.
4. With a craft knife, cutting mat, and ruler, cut starburst lines in the center of the motif.
5. Center the bobeche on the candlestick, then push in the candle. ❏

Folded Vellum Star Ornaments

These luminous star ornaments are made with vellum paper in a series of origami folds. They are very sturdy, and they look beautiful backlit in a window or in front of mini-lights on a tree.

Supplies

Paper and Adhesive

For a 5" star: Cut 5 pieces of rainbow or colored vellum 3-1/2" square. Cut 5 pieces of mounting adhesive 1-3/4" square.

For a 4" star: Cut 5 pieces of rainbow or colored vellum 3" square. Cut 5 pieces of mounting adhesive 1-1/2" square.

For a 3" star: Cut 5 pieces of rainbow or colored vellum 2-1/2" square. Cut 5 pieces of the mounting adhesive 1-1/4" square.

Tools and Other Supplies

Bone folder
Decorative edge scissors
Small hole punch
Thin metallic cord (9" for each ornament)

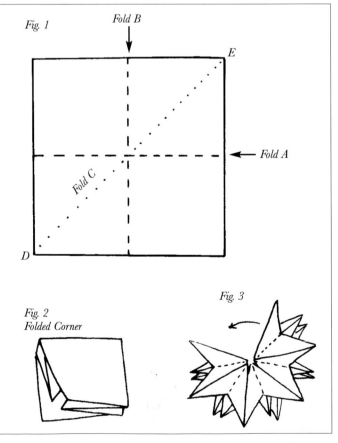

Fig. 1

Fold B

E

Fold A

Fold C

D

Fig. 2
Folded Corner

Fig. 3

Instructions

Folding

Follow these steps to fold each piece:

1. With the right side of the paper down, fold the page in half (Fold A). See Fig. 1.
2. Unfold. With the right side down, fold again in half, creating 4 equal sections (Fold B). See Fig. 1.
3. Turn the page over. With the right side up, make a diagonal fold corner to corner (Fold C). See Fig. 1.
4. Bring corners D and E together to create the fold.

Decorative Cutting

Use decorative edge scissors to cut along the inside folded edges on each piece to create a lacy effect. Make sure only the edges of the decorative motif cut through the folds.

Assembly

1. Glue all the pieces together with double-sided adhesive cut to fit. The folded corners should be on top of each other. (Fig. 2) When finished, the pieces will form a star when opened. (Fig. 3)
2. Make a hole in one point with a small hole punch.
3. Thread metallic cord through the hole to form the hanger. ❏

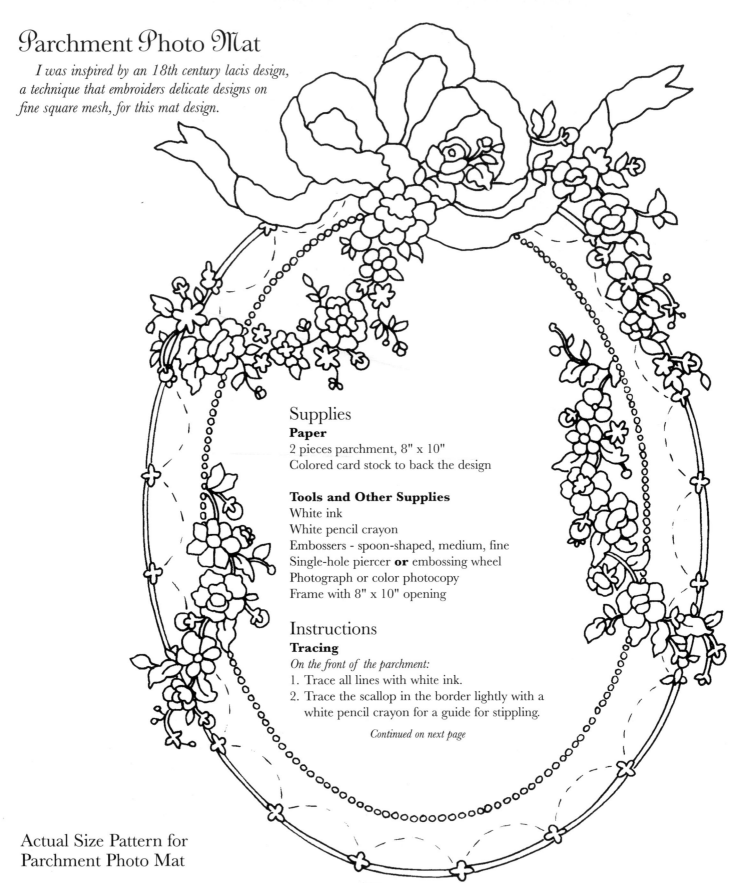

Parchment Photo Mat

I was inspired by an 18th century lacis design, a technique that embroiders delicate designs on fine square mesh, for this mat design.

Supplies

Paper
2 pieces parchment, 8" x 10"
Colored card stock to back the design

Tools and Other Supplies
White ink
White pencil crayon
Embossers - spoon-shaped, medium, fine
Single-hole piercer **or** embossing wheel
Photograph or color photocopy
Frame with 8" x 10" opening

Instructions

Tracing

On the front of the parchment:

1. Trace all lines with white ink.
2. Trace the scallop in the border lightly with a white pencil crayon for a guide for stippling.

Continued on next page

Actual Size Pattern for Parchment Photo Mat

Embossing

On the back of the parchment, on an embossing pad:

1. Emboss the bow and the large parts of the flowers and leaves with a spoon-shaped embosser.
2. Emboss all stems, flower centers, border motifs, and dots with a medium embosser.
3. With a fine embosser, emboss the small lines in the border design and the veins in the flowers.

Stippling

On the back of the parchment, on a piece of thin cardboard: With a single-hole piercer or embossing wheel, stipple the scalloped design in the border and on the bow.

Perforating

1. Pierce the inside edge of the oval to perforate. Remove.
2. Pierce around the floral garland to perforate. Separate.

Finishing

1. Cut the photo or photocopy to fit the oval mat. Position on the card stock and attach with double-sided tape.
2. Place a full sheet of parchment over the mounted photo.
3. Place the finished mat on top. Mount in a frame. ❑

Vellum Foldout Book

This little book contains a full sheet of vellum that unfolds to reveal an inspirational saying. It is modeled after a 15th century doctor's notebook that opened to reveal a vellum diagnostic chart. The suede paper has a soft, leather-like feel.

Supplies

Paper

Vellum, 8-1/2" x 11" (for the inside page)

2 medium weight mat boards, each 3-1/4" x 5" (for the front and back covers)

2 pieces decorative paper, 5-1/2" x 7" (for covering the mat board cover)

Suede paper, 2-1/2" x 9" (for the spine), 4-3/4" x 7" (for inside end papers)

Tools and Other Supplies

2 pieces of ribbon, each 6"

Stippling brush

Stamp pads in several colors

5-6 rubber stamps with classical motifs

Alphabet rubber stamp set for saying

Double-sided adhesive

Gold sealing wax and seal

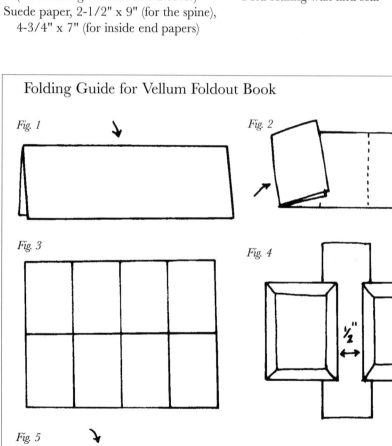

Folding Guide for Vellum Foldout Book

Fig. 1

Fig. 2

Fig. 3

Fig. 4

1/2"

Fig. 5

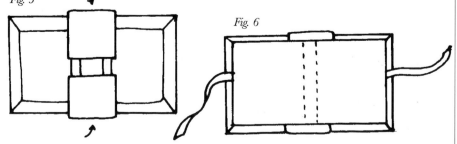

Fig. 6

INSTRUCTIONS

1. Cover the cover boards with decorative paper, using double-sided adhesive.
2. Stipple the vellum with stamp pad inks to make it look antique. Let dry.
3. Rubber stamp motifs and saying. Let dry.

Continued on next page

4. Fold the decorated vellum sheet in half horizontally. (Fig. 1) Accordion fold this half sheet into four 2-3/4" segments. (Fig. 2) Your folded vellum sheet will measure 2-3/4" x 4-1/4" and have eight segments. (Fig. 3) Set aside.

5. Cut pieces of double-sided adhesive the same sizes as the spine piece and the end paper pieces.

6. Adhere the spine to the covers. (Fig. 4) Fold over 2" at each end. (Fig. 5)

7. Place the ribbons on the inside covers. Adhere the end paper pieces into the insides of the covers. (Fig. 6)

8. With a piece of double-sided adhesive cut to 2-3/4" x 4-1/4", adhere the folded vellum page to the inside of the book.

9. Melt some sealing wax on the front of the book and press with the seal. ❑

Framed Parchment Sayings

The two sayings presented here are quick to do and very impressive when framed. The sayings fit in a frame with an 8" x 10" opening. I used inexpensive silver frames and glued charms at the corners to make them look more refined. "Little blessings make life a joy" is especially nice as a gift for a new baby. The name, date of birth, and parents' names can be added with white ink.

Supplies

Paper
Parchment, 8" x 10"
Optional: Sheets of printed colored vellum (They look especially nice mounted behind the parchment.)

Tools and Other Supplies
Picture frame with 8" x 10" opening
4 silver corner charms
White ink
White pencil crayon
Spoon-shaped embosser
Two-hole piercer
Single-hole piercer **or** embossing wheel

Instructions

Tracing
On the front of the parchment:
1. Trace all lines with white ink.
2. With a white pencil crayon, trace the dotted line for the cable border.

Embossing
On the back of the parchment, on an embossing pad:
1. Emboss all large areas and all the letters with a spoon-shaped embosser.
2. With a two-hole piercer, add the embossed cable design to the border.

Stippling
On the back of the parchment, on a piece of thin cardboard: With a single-hole piercer or embossing wheel, add the stippled design to all the areas of the design and the letters.

Finishing
Mount your finished piece in the frame.
❏

See page 110 for "Little Blessings" pattern.

Actual Size Pattern for "Listening Hearts" Framed Parchment Saying

Actual Size Pattern
for "Little Blessings"
Framed Parchment
Saying

Metric Conversion Chart

Inches to Millimeters and Centimeters

Inches	MM	CM
1/8	3	.3
1/4	6	.6
3/8	10	1.0
1/2	13	1.3
5/8	16	1.6
3/4	19	1.9
7/8	22	2.2
1	25	2.5
1-1/4	32	3.2
1-1/2	38	3.8
1-3/4	44	4.4
2	51	5.1
3	76	7.6
4	102	10.2
5	127	12.7
6	152	15.2
7	178	17.8
8	203	20.3
9	229	22.9
10	254	25.4
11	279	27.9
12	305	30.5

Yards to Meters

Yards	Meters
1/8	.11
1/4	.23
3/8	.34
1/2	.46
5/8	.57
3/4	.69
7/8	.80
1	.91
2	1.83
3	2.74
4	3.66
5	4.57
6	5.49
7	6.40
8	7.32
9	8.23
10	9.14

Index